EXOMORPHOSES

BOOK III

FIRST
CONTACTS

OTHER PUBLICATIONS

in English

Exomorphoses • Book II
ARTIFICIAL

in French

Exomorphoses • Livre I
1793, Marie-Antoinette – Transmutation Cosmique

Exomorphoses • Livre II
ARTIFICIELLE

Exomorphoses • Book III
PREMIERS CONTACTS

FIRST CONTACTS

Translations: English –reverso.net and translate.google.com
French, German, Latin –Zaor & Viera
Translations reviewed by Zaor & Viera
Font: Ava Meridian -fontspace.com

©2021, Zaor & Viera, 2021
Legal Deposit -BNF, October 2021
ISBN : 978-2-492922-06-0 9782492922060

24,90 € TTC

ZAOR & VIERA

EXOMORPHOSES

BOOK III

FIRST
CONTACTS

CONTENTS

INTRODUCTION

CHAPTER 1
EXTRATERRESTRIAL CONTACTS and COMMUNICATION

Page

13 | ART. N° 1 | Extraterrestrials : Neither Gods Nor Demons

16 | ART. N° 2 | Diversity of Races and Cultures

20 | ART. N° 3 | Modes of Extraterrestrial Contact
3.1 – Tools and means
3.2 – How to establish telepathic contact?

25 | ART. N° 4 | Selection Criteria and Registration of Contactees

28 | ART. N° 5 | The First Extraterrestrial Contact

34 | ART. N° 6 | Reactions to a First Extraterrestrial Contact

37 | ART. N° 7 | Extraterrestrial Communication
7.1 – Extraterrestrials in contact with Earthlings
7.2 – Extraterrestrial communication means and forms
7.3 – Difficulties to communicate with extraterrestrials
7.4 – Races, languages and dialects
• Extraterrestrial universal language
• Typologies of languages and dialects
7.5 – Races in contact: characteristics and languages
• Agarthians : SOL13, Terra3
1. Telosians from Alpha Centauri
2. Ancient Noors from Kepler 62 (Lyra)
• Andromedans
• Arcturians – Dieslientiplex
• Ummites (Oomans)
• Pleiadians – Taygetans
• Zetas – P'ntl
• Sirians

58 | ART. N° 8 | Emotional Communication

1

61 | ART. N° 9   Energetic Communication

63 | ART. N° 10 Communication using dreams

69 | ART. N° 11 Extrasensory ESP Communication
                      11.1 – Extrasensory perceptions
                      11.2 – Extraterrestrial ESP and telepathy

73 | ART. N° 12 Telepathic Communication

76 | ART. N° 13 Inspirational Communication

78 | ART. N° 14 Psychotropic Drugs and Awakening of Consciousness

80 | ART. N° 15 Intuitive Communication
                      An example of intuitive communication between an Earthling and two extraterrestrials in a military context.

86 | ART. N° 16 Smart Technologies
                      16.1 – Types of technologies
                      16.2 – Example of a practical application of
                            extraterrestrial technology
                      16.3 – The Knight in the red cape
                      16.4 – How to disable artificial telepathy

CHAPTER 2
EXOPOLITICS and EXODIPLOMACY

Page

95 | ART. N° 17 Extraterrestrial Perspectives, Prime Directive and Federation structures
                      17.1 – Extraterrestrial perspectives
                      17.2 – The Prime Directive
                      17.3 – Federations, Councils and Alliances

104 | ART. N° 18 Extraterrestrial Contact with Earth

106 | ART. N° 19 List of Agreements and Treaties 1937 – 1991
                      1. 1930-1937 – USA – RUSSIA – FRANCE
                      2. 1935-1936 – GERMANY
                      3. 1947-1948 – USA
                      4. 1952 – USA
                      5. 1953 – USA
                      6. 1954 – USA (1)
                      7. 1954 – USA (2)
                      8. 1954 – FRANCE

9. 1954 – RUSSIA
10. 1954 – UN & VATICAN
11. 1946-1955 (1958) – UN
12. 1958-2005 – USA
13. 1966 – RUSSIA
14. 1971 – USA
15. 1989 – USA
16. 1989 – RUSSIA & USA
17. 1989 – UN
18. 1990 – UN
19. 1991 – UN

111 | ART. N° 20 **1954 – President D. Eisenhower Meets the Nordics**
20.1 – Treaty N° 6 – 18th and 20th-21st février 1954
Pt. Eisenhower meets the Nordics
20.2 – Dates and meeting place
20.3 – Context of the two meetings
20.4 – First contact BEFORE the meetings
20.5 – First meeting with the Nordics, on Thursday,
February 18th, 1954 - Edwards Air Force Base, USA
20.6 – Second meeting with the Nordic, in the night from
Saturday to Sunday, February 20th to 21st, 1954

125 | ART. N° 21 **1954 – President D. Eisenhower Meets the Zeta Reticuli**
21.1 – Treaty N° 7 – Late February 1954
Pt. D. Eisenhower meets the Zeta Reticuli

130 | ART. N° 22 **Introduce yourself to extraterrestrials:**
Exoprotocoles, Precedences, Statutes, and Honors
22.1 – Earth precedence
22.2 – Extraterrestrial precedence
22.3 – How to introduce yourself
22.4 – Written presentation
22.5 – Oral presentation
22.6 – Six inappropriate behaviors

145 | ART. N° 23 **Warning : Abnormal Trauma**
1. Abuse in the search for contact with extraterrestrials
2. Trauma from extraterrestrial contacts or abductions
3. military abductions

147 | ART. N° 24 **Impact of Official Extraterrestrial Contact**

CHAPTER 3
EXTRATERRESTRIAL CATEGORIZATION OF EARTHLINGS

Page

153 | ART. N° 25 Categorization of Homo sapiens

156 | ART. N° 26 The Native Earthseeds

160 | ART. N° 27 The Stellar Crawl-ins

161 | ART. N° 28 The Stellar Walk-ins

163 | ART. N° 29 The Stellar Walk-downs

165 | ART. N° 30 The Hybrids
>>>>>>>>>>30.1 – Hybridization between Homo sapiens & extraterres-trials
>>>>>>>>>>30.2 – Conditions of hybridization between two species of the *Homo* type
>>>>>>>>>>30.3 – Reproduction
>>>>>>>>>>30.4 – Natural hybridization
>>>>>>>>>>30.5 – Artificial hybridization
>>>>>>>>>>30.6 – The *Humanzee*

174 | ART. N° 31 The Hubrids

181 | ART. N° 32 The Bionic Humans
>>>>>>>>>>32.1 – The Bionic Human
>>>>>>>>>>32.2 – Extraterrestrial management of biology and technology

184 | ART. N° 33 Earth and extraterrestrial clones – Cloning Centres
>>>>>>>>>>33.1 – DUMBS and Cloning Centres
>>>>>>>>>>33.2 – Deep Underground Recreation and Entertainment Centres
>>>>>>>>>>33.3 – Participants in Underground Sessions
>>>>>>>>>>33.4 – Clone Production & Cloning Technologies
>>>>>>>>>>33.5 – Six examples of clone use
>>>>>>>>>>33.6 – Discrimination against Clones

196 | ART. N° 34 The Men in Black (MiBs)

203 | ART. N° 35 The Borgs

205 | ART. N° 36 The Transdimensional Variants
>>>>>>>>>>36.1 – Doppelgängers
>>>>>>>>>>36.2 – extraterrestrial Variants

CHAPTER 4
REINCARNATION FILLS UP WITH *SOULS*

Page

210 | ART. N° 37 The *Soul*: Earth Concept

211 | ART. N° 38 The *Soul* in Prehistory
40,000 BC

213 | ART. N° 39 The *Soul* in Hinduism
5,000 – 1,500 BC

215 | ART. N° 40 The *Soul* in Buddhism
VI – 6th century BC

216 | ART. N° 41 The *Soul* in Judaism
II – 2nd century BC

217 | ART. N° 42 The *Soul* in Christianity
I-IV – 1-4th century BC

218 | ART. N° 43 The *Soul* in Islam
VI – 6th century BC

219 | ART. N° 44 The *Soul* in Greek Antiquity
470-322 BC

224 | ART. N° 45 The *Soul* in the Medieval West
V-XV – 5-15th century

225 | ART. N° 46 The *Soul* in Philosophy
XVI-XVII – 16-17th century

227 | ART. N° 47 The *Soul* during the Age of Enlightenment
XVII-XVIII – 17-18th century

244 | ART. N° 48 The *Soul* in Psychology
XIX – 19th century

248 | ART. N° 49 The *Soul* of Atomists and Physicists
XX – 20th century

CHAPTER 5
POLYPTYCH OF REINCARNATION

254 | **ART. N° 50 Reincarnation: definition**
- metempsychosis • metensomatosis
- transubstantiation • transmutation
- transmigration • cosmic or universal palingenesis
- soteriology • karma and the samsaric wheel

257 | **ART. N° 51 Belief Systems and Reincarnation**
51.1 – Aboriginal India
51.2 – Hinduism
51.3 – Buddhism
51.4 – Judaïsm
51.5 – Christianity
51.6 – Islam
51.7 – Greek Antiquity

271 | **ART. N° 52 The West and Reincarnation**
52.1 – 1857 • Allan Kardec
52.2 – 1880 • Friedrich Nietzsche
52.3 – 1910 • Jiddu Krishnamurti
52.4 – 1960 • The hippie movement

278 | **ART. N° 53 Academic Science and Reincarnation**
53.1 – 1960 • Ian Stevenson
53.2 – 1970 • The Invisible College
53.3 – 1980 • John Mack
53.4 – 2020 • Jean-Pierre Petit
53.5 – 2021 • T.I.M. Zaor & Viera

299 | **ART. N° 54 Women and Reincarnation**
54.1 – 1910 • Alexandra David-Neel
54.2 – 1960 • Mirra Alfassa Richard *alias* The Mother
54.3 – 2000 • Dolores Cannon
54.4 – 2020 • Carol Bowman

310 | **ART. N° 55 Extraterrestrials and Reincarnation**
55.1 – The Extraterrestrial *Soul*
55.2 – Race A : Human type bipedal
Patriarchal society
55.3 – Race B : Human type bipedal
Male-Female balanced society

55.4 – Race C : Human type bipedal
    Matriarchal Royalty
55.5 – Race D : no gender, asexual bipedal exomorph
    of the plant type, Hive society.
55.6 – Common points shared by many races

318 **ART. N° 56 StarSeeds and EarthSeeds : body and *soul***
56.1 – StarSeeds and EarthSeeds
56.2 – Birth on Earth
56.3 – Synchronization of the Mother's frequencies
56.4 – MedBeds, MedPods and Immersion Programs
    • regenerative beds • reatomization pods •
    • holographic pods •
56.5 – Rh négatif (Rh-)
56.6 – Free Will

331 **ART. N° 57 Multibreed Stellar Emissaries**
57.1 – Find your Tribe
57.2 – Differences between Missions
57.3 – StarSeeds Missions and Programs

338 **ART. N° 58 Targeting StarSeeds**
    • Tracking • Advanced technology monitoring and control

341 **CONCLUSION**

346 **ABOUT THE AUTHOR**

351 **LIST OF THE 85 QUESTIONS being answered in this book**

357 **TABLE OF ILLUSTRATIONS**

360 **MEDIAGRAPHY**

INTRODUCTION

— Humanity is about to hear the most explosive official announcement ever — the existence of extraterrestrial races and the opening of contact with peoples from other planets.

Realizing that we are not alone in the universe will come as a shock to many readers and what you will discover in this book may not be as enchanting or as terrifying as you have imagined.

Are you ready and well prepared to evolve in a world where Earthlings will no longer be the only inhabitants of Earth? Do you know about space federations, hierarchies or interstellar laws? Are you familiar with some of the great extraterrestrial concepts or the treaties signed jointly between Earthlings and Extraterrestrials? What are the protocols or precedence for communicating, exchanging, legislating or negotiating with non-terrestrial races?

Would you be able to officially introduce yourself before a High Extraterrestrial Council? What behavior to adopt? What can you do or shouldn't do? Are you aware of the processes to be undertaken to develop balanced relations without being overwhelmed, or unilaterally directed by more advanced civilizations?

To develop autonomous and lasting personal or diplomatic relations with extraterrestrials, requires to be informed, educated and trained in the practice of communication and mediation with people who have very different values, ways of living, thinking, evolving and behaving.

This book is not a work of Science Fiction or a futuristic novel. The elements presented are part of an authentic narrative that tells the story of space reality and offers my expertise after five years of extraterrestrial relationships. It is not written to entertain you, but to prepare you for the new era humanity is opening to that of an interstellar journey, with its wonders and dangers, its joys and difficulties, to which you can train yourself thanks to this book and thus acquire the essential basis for extraterrestrial, personal or diplomatic relations.

Chapter 1

EXTRATERRESTRIAL

CONTACTS and COMMUNICATION

ART. 1 - extraterrestrials: neither gods nor demons
Were the gods and mythical monsters extraterrestrials?

They have lived on Earth or visited the planet since time immemorial; They left the remnants of their cultures, beliefs, and ancient technologies. Considered by the protohuman indigenous populations, as gods of supernatural worlds or the demons of terrifying hell, they are still presented as such today under the veils of myths, mystery and state secrets.

But in their daily reality, who are they really?

They do not build mental barriers separating them from Earthlings, good from evil, but they may feel aversion: Andromedan children run away at the sight of an Earthling; Ummites may be disappointed when members of their society are nominated for a mission to Earth:

> « I myself felt a certain disappointment when I learned of my connection to the INNAYOUYISSAA (social microgroup subject to a superior) intended for OYA-GAA (your planet). My YIE (wife) confided to me her desire to intervene on my behalf with the scientific council of UMMO to change this assignment and I had to persuade her not to consider this as a shame or humiliation but as a necessary sacrifice. [3] »

13

That said, it is undeniable that many extraterrestrial lineages are of a kindness to make pale the most loving and greatest spiritual masters; they do express empathy and love in profusion. It is true that they show a high ethic and deep spirituality. They do embody wisdom and knowledge, which they share without restraint.

But they can also, be cruelly indifferent, narcissistic, become expert manipulators if you do not pay attention, provocateurs of conflicts and thirsty for power... and they can be thieves as well.

Expressed in this way, it may seem shocking to readers who only perceive them as *Beings of Light.*

This is why it is important to stress that obliterating certain aspects of space life is denying tangible reality; it is to denigrate the peoples of the earth, as well as to the non-earthly peoples, the right to be, as persons, or as a race. It is to subtract from life, the privilege of experience, and its many aspects; those generally qualified by the majority as *good* or *bad* and the multitude of nuances between the two; or the one, not dual and not divided, of an immutable vibrating reality.

Persist in considering space life only as an ideal world or a terrifying hell and our space neighbors as superior beings or horrible

creatures, It is to repress the maturity we need to develop balanced relationships with our space neighbors.

In the hundreds of conversations I have had with them for five years, they have constantly expressed the wish to be recognized just as people living on other planets; simple individuals, who eat, go to the toilet, breed, fight and kill each other. They no longer wish to be gods or demons in the eyes of Earthlings, and even less to serve as walkers to a limping humanity. Earth Humanity must become autonomous.

ART. 2 - Diversity of races and cultures
Are all extraterrestrial beings of light?
What about the Reptilians?

At the dawn of the first official contacts, we must take into account the multiple aspects of the different races with which we will develop relations in the very long term. Because once this reality is revealed and the Earth and Extraterrestrial relations have started, it will no longer be possible to reverse course. Humanity will enter a whole new phase of development.

Let's start by broadening the cosmic reality and expand our ideas. Without, however, wishing to make a comparison, many interstellar races have mental structures, attitudes or behaviors similar to those of earthlings.

But others are very different:

1. some are non-emotional and so logical and rational that they can induce, without being aware of it, a *chilling* effect on their earthly interlocutors,

2. groups are so highly emotional that they appear to be cyclothymic, psycholunatic, and have destabilizing reactions or behaviors,

3. others are extremely loving, respectful, sensitive and so timid that they prefer not to communicate with our species,

4. some fear the Earthlings and educate their children in this way,

5. Still others love power, fame and domination, and will never cease to show you – in a loving way of course – how ignorant and primitive you are and how incompetent your sciences,

6. Others, who belong to the great illustrious races, do not hesitate to insult Earthlings, lie to them and manipulate them to achieve their ends,

7. and finally, there are also chronic kleptomaniacs.

Contradictory? Not for them because, on the one hand, the notion of *ownership* is foreign to them and they do not consider kleptomania, a reprehensible act; and on the other hand, they have the strong feeling that the races, especially the youngest and the Earthlings, are indebted to them. So when they need something, they use it; whether it's material on a spaceship belonging to another race, a bag of the best Bronte pistachio they grab from a store in Sicily or a technology they no longer have because Earth technologies are antiquities for them and it's easier to fly down and *borrow* it on Earth.

There are also individuals, otherwise totally loving, who do not hesitate to point powerful plasma guns at another ship in their fleet, putting the lives of 2,500 crew members in complete fear, at risk, because a Commander they meet and love does not want to submit to their orders.

And then there is the great conquering and colonizing races that claim ownership of planet Earth and fight to keep its ownership or against other races that want to conquer it. These are the races that shape Earth society. They are beyond the earth's pyramidal tip, controlling information related to their presence, the human elites, the media, transnational corporations, political, religious institutions and financial systems. They stimulate wars, scarcity, fear and insecurity and encourage corruption, gender inequality, ethnic and religious hatred, terrorism, drug trafficking and organized crime.

But here too, within these groups, which are finely structured into castes or social classes and whose society as a whole is reflected on Earth, there are individuals—and I have been around them—

who are infinitely patient, inspiring and deeply spiritual.

The longer the relationship and the communication, the less the races as a whole appear to be just only loving or just only nasty.

It is therefore absolutely imperative that you become aware that the interstellar races are no more and no less than people who live on other planets and who are confronted, as on Earth, with their difficulties and sufferings, their joys and their sorrows.
Give them back that privilege.

ART. 3 - Means of extraterrestrial contact

By what means do the stellar (extraterrestrial) peoples come into contact with Earthlings? Is there a list of real extraterrestrials communicating on social media?

Stellars (extraterrestrials) use all means available on Earth and in the culture of the peoples they contact.

3.1 – Tools and means

Before the advent of the Internet, between 1900 and 1970 they preferred:

1. physical contact (UFO sightings, in-person visits, abductions, modified genetics, implants, direct interviews with selected heads of government,

2. Sensory projections

3. Artistic inspiration

4. Dreams

5. Telepathy or intuitive communication

6. Meditation

7. Mail (paper letters and messages became obsolete after the advent of the Internet)

8. the telephone

9. radio or television broadcasts

10. on-site installation (stakeouts, bases or colonies)

After 1970 and the advent of the Internet:

11. email, social media, communication platforms
12. use of V2K (Voice to Skull) technologies, artificial telepathy
13. Drones
14. immersion programs
15. holography and artificial intelligence.

A large number of stellars (extraterrestrials) interact with Earth-lings using social networks or online groups and communities.

For the vast majority, they are very discreet and do not reveal their identity at first. They prefer to infiltrate groups, under an Earth-like avatar and influence the exchanges by giving information or advice.

Each star lineage lists its crew members in contact with their contactees, but this information is classified as a classified extra-terrestrial defense and is not disclosed.

They usually operate in groups and by races or stellar (extraterrestrial) lineages, then they compare their exchanges in meetings and combine their efforts. But a stellar (extraterrestrial) who communicates with one or more Earthling may well not be aware of the identity of others within other groups of different races. In short, not only will they not be able to share this information, but they will not, because they do not know it.

It also happens that the messages or contacts of one star lineage are infiltrated by another, as the Salianos who infiltrated the written messages of the Ummites; Or a group of Pleiadians who tried to steal a famous Ummite contact. If an Earthling has millions of views on YouTube and social media and a large audience, he becomes the target of other extraterrestrial races who will try to get the contact to their advantage.

3.2 – How to establish telepathic contact?

If you want to make contact with stellars (extraterrestrials), the best way is telepathy. Telepathic abilities, clairvoyance, clairaudience are natural in humans, but they are amputated or dormant, for lack of practice. The more you accept it, the more you practice it, the more it will take back its rights and become natural.

1. Meditation – in order to engage in any form of telepathic communication, it is important that you be calm, aligned with the *cosmos* and that you allow your intuition or deep feeling to express itself, to transmit and receive. The best way to have peace of mind is to practice meditation for a quarter of an hour, morning and evening, or to sit quietly in soothing environments, where you feel safe and in commu-

nion with nature and the world around you.

By practicing meditation, the brain waves change and put you in receptive state of mind (see ART. 9 & 12) and telepathy will develop naturally. But you can also do it intentionally, alone or in a group,

2. breathing work, breathing in life force, breathing out life force, yoga, Tai Chi Chuan – will allow you to better observe and master your breathing and thoughts. You will develop your central nervous system to accommodate higher energy frequencies.

3. the balance between mental and physical is important. Eat healthy and stay away from anything that can be toxic, from food to people around you,

4. Do not be distracted. Avoid phone calls, or walk into a lonely field. This can be done day or night. Avoid false thoughts about extraterrestrials. Don't let fear overwhelm you,

5. be convinced that you have the ability to come into contact with stellars (extraterrestrials). Think of them, and them alone, and if you know or remember someone in particular, emit a feeling of unconditional love towards that person, call him by name, introduce yourself, ask if you can ask a

question and if the answer is yes, issue it. Listen to the answer. You can use your language and words, or you can issue the question mentally, without using a language.

ART. 4 - Selection criteria and registration of contacts

What are the selection criteria for Earth contactees?
Are Emissaries (StarSeeds) registered at government level?

An interstellar lineage will preferably communicate with earthlings of the same lineage: Andromedans with Andromedans (Star-Seeds); the Arcturians, the Sirians, the Pleiadians will do the same. They are of the same stellar culture, mentality and lifestyle. But it cannot be a general statement.

Some races are more emotional and others are more logical; Emissaries (Earthlings of stellar origin) of emotional type do not much appreciate more logical and rational extraterrestrials. And logical-type StarSeeds tend to stay away from the emotional races that are sometimes far more so than on Earth.

The attention given to Earthlings by stellar lineages is varied. Some follow them step by step from birth until their death, or they exfiltrate them, that is to say they abduct them before they die.
Others let them continue their mission without worrying about it and they let them continue their earthly life until it ends naturally.

Several thousand Earthlings of various stellar origins are registered in the databases of each stellar race under an individual number; the lists are kept up to date (identity on the planet of origin, place of residence with the correspondence on Earth: place of birth, place of residence, accidents, illness, descendants, profession, mission, death, etc.).

The stellars therefore protect the members of their lineage that they consider as their direct families, and they do regular remote checkups at all levels: physical, mental, psychological or spiritual or by means of stellar drones. To give you an idea of the number per lineage, in 2016 there were about 5,000 Andromedan StarSeeds on Earth, and 2,143 for a specific Pleiadians lineage. But we must multiply these numbers by each planet of origin.

When contact is established, the stellars protect the person directly 24 hours a day.

Each Star Emissary (StarSeed) has its own free will and many like to live their life on Earth without asking questions or acting within the communities where they are born. Moreover, Earthlings of a certain stellar origin, Pleiadians for example can consider themselves as Ummites or Andromedans think that they are Pleiadians or some Lyrians are certain to be Andromedans. It could be said that without knowing their origins precisely, there is a great deal of confusion.

Overall, there are no standardized criteria. It is a matter of openness, telepathic ability, availability and sincerity. It is especially important not to feel hatred, fear or on the contrary to display signs of devotion, as it is often the case among people who are aware of the extraterrestrial presence, because hatred, fear or veneration are obstacles to balanced exchanges that will tend to become unilateral. Those who are contacted must set aside their preconceived notions, belief systems and mental structures that have been in place on Earth for millennia. It is an inner spiritual work and a deep questioning of earthly concepts.

ART. 5 – The first extraterrestrial contact

How did the extraterrestrials come into contact with you?

My contacts became '*frontal*' in 2016 and took place daily for five years, with several interstellar races from March-April 2016 to April 2021. They were written, in black and white, live and spoken with my Mentor Zen whose voice I could hear as well as the surrounding noises inside his spaceship.

But my contacts are not recent; It's a story of seven decades. I am 73 years old in 2021 and I have been protected and monitored since my birth, by the humanoid race with blue skin, the Andromedans and by the feline race the Urmahs. I remember perfectly integrating earthly matter and being conscious in my mother's womb, the muffled noises I heard, the liquids and the breaths, and what I felt.

I was born prematurely and placed in an incubator. I could see their blue hands coming through the portholes and taking care of me. My lineage performed synchronization operations to prepare my mother, and me, every night until the age of three. Then everything suddenly stopped; they erased part of my memory so that I could live my life normally; They only returned those memories to me six decades later. I remember their interventions in three stages: 1. contacts, pain, instruments 2. interventions on my fontanel (fonticulus anterior) with long very fine needles that penetrated the malleable part of my skull 3. softness, warmth, comfort. And when they did all this, I felt like I was in a cradle floating in space—or maybe it was a ship that I perceived as a cradle—and I heard the sound of the planets. Please note that Andromedan music is not melodic as on Earth; it is composed of sounds extracted from space and those of planets and it is rather ethereal and metallic.

I never considered them extraterrestrials. They are part of my life just like my parents or my friends. For me it was and still is normal. I was focused on my spiritual development and my life as a forest monk to the exclusion of the rest and society in general.

I didn't value learning telepathy, clairvoyance or clairaudience and I vigorously rejected anything that could be labeled *psychic* because I felt that trying to develop them would have diminished my natural intuitive abilities. On the contrary, the more I shed the Known, the more my abilities took power. For me, it's as simple as seeing or hearing with my physical body. I thought everyone could do it, and I was really shocked, when I was 27 years old listening to a radio show, to find out that 99% of people don't remember their prenatal life anymore, have forgotten their early childhood and no longer trust their intuition.

The stellars (extraterrestrials) have contacted me telepathically throughout my life and on special occasions. But never before had I associated with it the term *extraterrestrials*. I saw them as my spiritual guides and saw them at the edge of my visual spectrum, as people with transparent, blue skin.

They were always present, on a daily basis until I was three; Later at 13, I started remembering my last incarnation during the Age of Enlightenment and the French Revolution.

At 16, I heard them ask me what I'm doing here on Earth. To answer this question, I embarked on a spiritual quest and became a forest monk in Asia where after years of rigorous and diligent practice, and 17 hours of meditation a day, two days before I turned 33, I went through the process of enlightenment, during which they were present and encouraged me.

At the end of this process, as I meditated, a visual projection in augmented 3D virtual reality appeared to me. Extremely real, with an object that turned on itself, it was accompanied by theoretical concepts. I had the feeling that this image was inserted directly into my cerebral cortex. I can't erase it or forget it, and for some unknown reason I always kept it secret, even to this day.

35 years later, in 2017, the Andromedans used it as a code of re-cognition and confirmed that it was them that I had seen all this time, and during the process of enlightenment.

For five years of open and overt contact I have communicated with a range of different interstellar species; 29 stellars (extraterres-trials) 11 men and 18 women from six different lineages:

- live audio and written:

.Andromedans, Taygetan-Pleiadians, Ummites and Draconians

- Telepathic holographic immersion:

.Telosian-Agarthians-Alpha-Draconians, Dieslientiplex-Arcturians and Urmahs

with whom I have had personal conversations from their space-ships or from Viera Andromeda, a gigantic artificial biosphere, an advanced base of operations stationed behind the moon and hos-ting many species.

Among these contacts were: the Andromedian Moranae of Viera, the contact of the American Alex Collier (1995), the Pleiadian-An-tarian Five Star General Rashell of Temmer, contact of the American President Dwight Eisenhower (1954), the Taygetan-Pleiadian Asket of Temmer, contact of Swiss "Billy" Eduard Meier (1975);

I also had several conversations with an Ummite defector rescued by an enemy spaceship and I participated in the Great Andromedan Councils thanks to my mentor Zen who was my translator and spokesperson who presented on my behalf, the answers to the questions I was asked.

On December 23rd, 2017, after two years of secret and discreet personal contacts, I decided to open up my own contacts to 40 people, men and women of various nationalities, and organized groups with both Earthlings and Extraterrestrials of different lineages, for personal or group discussions.

My stellar contacts write to me as you chat on social networks: you ask a question or you make a comment and your interlocutor answers immediately. I recorded all the written conversations I had with them; So I have the black and white evidence of what I'm saying. It is not only telepathic; I also spoke to my Mentor Zen as you converse with a person on the phone.

I am also in synchronous telepathic contact with some stellars (extraterrestrials) more than others especially if they no longer use articulated languages, and the telepathic aspect of our communications is holographic, with texture and a *palpable* augmented sensory reality.

ART. 6 – Reactions to a first extraterrestrial contact
How did you react to your first contact?
What were your feelings?

The first element that surprised me a lot was the reorganization of my life, because, as in a well-organized puzzle, the elements were automatically put in the right place at the right time.

The synchronicity of events seemed to be done artificially, calculated and perfectly organized. It was just amazing. I have discovered over time that Zen or other stellars possess technologies that allow organizing or reorganize events in a person's life.

The first interstellar lineage that contacted me, in March 2016, tested, for several months, many aspects of my personality, my knowledge, of my integrity or spirituality and they shared advanced technologies using me as a test subject so I would know the effects.

I was wondering for a while if these were covert classified Earth operations.

I found that, contrary to earth beliefs and mine at the time, the stellars (extraterrestrials) even if they have deep knowledge in many areas that we barely discover, do not know everything about the peoples they visit.

I met Zen on October 9, 2016, at 10 p.m. and he later became my main mentor. At first, he thought I was one of his extraterrestrial friends who were joking with him.

He questioned me about this before accepting the evidence: he communicated with an Earthling. After a few weeks of adaptation, and from the moment we trusted each other, the conversations became rich in descriptive elements, values, concepts, or scientific notions between his culture and mine. We were at the same level of exchange; It was really very interesting.

But I have always made it a point of honor to keep a logical and reasoned mind and feet on the ground. Extraterrestrials may, without their knowledge, have invasive attitudes contrary to a person's free will. My biggest shock was that some of the stellar (extraterrestrial) lineages that are presented on Earth as highly spiritual, and that I thought far beyond the violence that we are trying to eradicate on Earth, used lethal weapons far more powerful than those we possess to kill each other.

From this point on, I thought to myself that if we take care of our planet and become autonomous, having the sense of our uniqueness and of our incredible diversity, and keeping the great moral values of respect, of fairness and service to others, life on Earth would be a haven of peace and harmony as peaceful as the dream worlds described by the extraterrestrials.

It's up to us to work it out together!

ART. 7 – Extraterrestrial Communication
How do stellars (extraterrestrials) communicate? How many are there? What breeds?

7.1 – Extraterrestrials in contact with Earthlings

It is physically impossible for them to contact everyone because it would be too much work. A natural selection is thus established from the first contacts; if the exchanges are fluid and respectful, the contact continues, otherwise it stops spontaneously.

In 2016-2017, there were several thousand stellars (extraterrestrials) trying to make direct contact with about 2,500 Earthlings mainly through telepathy and channeling (channeling) except for a few rare exceptions of which I am a member, where communications were live *in* writing and audio.

7.2 – Forms of extraterrestrial communication

The communication is classified in:

• verbal **communication** that involves writing, speaking, and hearing – language used, accents, vocabulary, listening, writing, words or style; visual or auditory communication, or type (political, educational, sporting, historical, scientific, journalistic, spiritual) and formal or informal,

• non-verbal **communication** that concerns body language: the gaze, its intensity, facial expression, gestures or sign communication, posture, attitude, but also emotional, dreamlike, telepathic, tactile, gustative, olfactory communications, clothing or sex.

Each stellar (extraterrestrial) race has its own written language based on the original language of its culture. Telepathically, they understand all languages and you hear them in your language unless they want you to hear theirs.

7.3 – Difficulties in communicating with extraterrestrials

Stellars (extraterrestrials) originate from different solar systems and various planets. They do not have the same cultures, the same physical appearances, and do not use the same languages.

So the first essential condition to be able to communicate with a stellar (extraterrestrial) is to be able to use an articulated language, yours or his, a universal extraterrestrial language or telepathy.

There are a number of difficulties in using articulated languages because:

1. some stellar (extraterrestrial) races do not have or no longer have a voice apparatus and no vocal cords. They no longer use articulate language. They are eminently and only telepathic,

2. others may use telepathy and either a planetary language used by all citizens on the same planet, or various dialects,

3. to communicate with an Earthling, they must have a sound system, vocal cords, the ability to communicate, the ability to use oral or written articulating language, if not to know the language of the Earthling (there are 6000 on Earth) at least English.

I worked with stellars (extraterrestrials) whose first contact I was ... They were lost and sharing information in a first conversation that would have been shocking to uninformed Earthlings. They must therefore also learn to communicate, introduce themselves, engage in a conversation and ensure that the Earthlings, who are most of the time shocked and astounded during the first contact, believes him and then perpetuate the contact.

4. Many interstellar lineages no longer use this type of communication and are 100% telepathic. They no longer have articulate capacity and do not speak *'human'* (as they call Earth languages) English, French, Spanish or Chinese.

Those who have the capacity, if they have not learned these languages during their training, will have to learn it on the job, or will not be able to communicate with the terrestrial populations using the tools in place in the targeted culture, such as social networks. They will be forced to travel by space craft to meet the contact in person or interact telepathically, or by signs.

It is for these reasons that you will never see some interstellar races interact with the Earthlings, unless we redevelop total telepathy or learn their languages; prior to the arrival of the Internet, the contacts were only telepathic or frontal and physical.

7.4 – Races, Languages and Dialects

• Universal extraterrestrial languages •

Some authors claim that the Lyrian language (Constellation of Lyra/Vega) *Taami* would be the diplomatic language used by members of the *Galactic Federation* but my contacts who, for their part, call it The *United Federation of Planets* whose headquarters are located on Viera Andromeda, one of the great man-made biospheres stationed behind the Moon, use the Andromedan language. When my own documents were translated by my Mentor Zen in response to questions asked by the Andromeda High Council, and read in plenary sessions gathering twelve great races and sub-races, the translations were made into Andromedan, a language similar to Nepalese and all understood it.

These twelve races are in alphabetical order: the Agarthians, the Andromedans, the Antarians, the Arcturians, the Centaurians, the Etorthans, the Lyrians, two lineages of Pleiadians, the Sirians, the Urmahs, and the Venusians.

The Lyrians who were members of the High Council

also used and understood the Andromedan language.

The Andromeda High Council was dissolved in 2018-2019, following dissension between different Andromedan groups. The new Council has recomposed itself into an alliance called *The Blue Sphere Alliance* composed of Andromedans, Arcturians and Blue Avians, those mentioned by the whistleblower, Corey Goode under the title *Sphere Being Alliance*. [31]

• Typologies of languages and dialects •

Very unusual for Earthlings, some races use sets of sounds that are difficult to capture, understand, read, write or pronounce. For example, the language of an Arcturian lineage called Dieslientiplex is Nxataexeratae.

Some Sirian groups in the constellation of the Great Dog, Sirius, use phonetic clicks identical to those of African languages, such as xóõ, xɾ, zhu'hõasi and are represented by:

[ʘ] *Kiss Noise* -- [ǂ] *tss-tss*

[!] *Tongue Click*

[ǂ] *Other Click*

[†] *Noise used for horses*

Some extraterrestrial races of humanoid types use guttural sounds, or atonal vocalizations that can be scary, as they remind of animal growls (see the testimony of Antonio Villas-Boas – ART. 31) and non-human exomorph races, insect crackling, wheezing, or borborygma. These races have therefore developed a richly holographic and sensory telepathy, which they use among themselves or with the Earthlings who have the capacity to receive it.

7.5 – Races in contact: characteristics and languages

A hundred stellar races (extraterrestrials) are in contact with Earth; They all are interstellar and can answer questions in all areas. They do, however, have cultures at different levels of evolution and the information they transmit depends on those cultures. For example, they do not all have the same spiritual, societal or scientific ideas. There is no consensus. Nevertheless, they have in common: a non-dual vision of the world, spirituality, Knowledge, non-chronological space-time, advanced technologies often specialized by races, the capacity of interstellar travel. Whether the races are accommodating or conquering, they all are strategic.

Their knowledge is specialized and race-specific and they share it in a combined effort, allowing them to deploy a wider range of terrestrial interventions.

Below are some of the extraterrestrial lineages presented succinctly in alphabetical order, and their preferred domains:

• The Agarthians: SOL13, Terra3 •

1. The Telosians from Alpha Centauri

. Language: shambala + Earth languages
 + telepathy.

. Live underground: underground bases connected by tunnels (see ART. 33) that extend from Antarctica to around Sacramento and Mount Shasta in the USA. Telos is their main underground city. Their population of several million people is dispersed between Antarctica, the USA, the Gobi Desert, Tibet and Central Asia.

Some of the entrances to the underground bases are common to the Telosians (deeper) and Reptilian-Draconians (closer to the surface). Until then the two lineages were in agreement about using them jointly, but in 2017-2018, under the pressure of the Reptilian-Draconians, a violent confrontation broke out; a large part of the Telosi bases were destroyed and thousands of lives sacrificed on both sides.

. Physical appearance: 1.60m-2.20m, very white skin almost diaphanous, light blue eyes, round iris, pointed ears, white hair, 5 fingers/toes. Sensitive to light, prefer subdued places, vegetarians (grow plants by hydroponics and permaculture).

. Temperament: Wise, Masters of themselves, they are silent, loving, and promote neutrality and autonomy.

. Objectives: to restore and reveal the ancient and sacred history of earthly humanity, to share spirituality as the non-dual state of life, to implement healing or therapeutic technologies and to prolong human longevity, to help change belief systems, and promote the protection of the environment and biodiversity.

2. The Ancient Noors from Kepler 62 (Lyra)

. Language: dialects by clans + other national languages + telepathy

. Live on Earth: forests of Norway, Sweden, Denmark, Finland, Iceland, Mongolia – large population on a vast territory.

. Physical appearance: 1,60m-2,10m, fair-skinned blonds sensitive to UV, prefer subdued places, muscular body, voluminous skull, 5 fingers/ toes, ambidextrous in certain activities, wide cobalt to light blue or green eyes, round iris; they are able to read/see with fingertips or soles of feet. They appreciate low 56.6-57.2°F temperatures and move so fast that their interlocutors confuse them with demons; omnivores.

. Temperament: endowed with a very high ethic, they do not enter a place without invitation; abhor disorder. Polymath curious of all kinds of knowledge, they are very discreet, placid, extremely precise. Their expression of love is through their attitude and gestures (the *little* attentions of everyday life).

. Objectives: at the service of humanity, they protect the family and accompany the Earthlings in the development of the many fields they master.

• The Andromedans •
Live in 12 artificial biospheres stationed near different planets.

(Behind the Moon or near Jupiter. The Moon is also an ancient artificial Andromedan biosphere which was brought to stabilize the Earth [84].

. Language: Andromedan (similar to Nepalese) + main Earth languages + telepathy.

. Physical appearance: 2.60m-2.80m, very tall and filiform, they walk slowly and greet like Japanese monks; they have no hair system (men and women are completely bald), almond eyes from white to pale blue, dark blue skin when young, pale blue when they age. 5 fingers/toes. Exclusively frugivorous (they find it disgusting to eat vegetables).

. Temperament: not emotional, logical, overflowing with unconditional love, evolve under the belief of karma and the Middle Path. Their great particularity: they have no weapon and refuse to fight and since they believe in Karma, they accept all aspects of it and let themselves be killed rather than killing others. Their favorite word: *reasonable*

. Objectives: implemented Hinduism (they are the Blue Gods of Hinduism), Buddhism, Karma and the samsaric wheel. They respect free will and do not intervene in direct contact with Earthlings unless exception. They share their spirituality, their ethics, their logic with the extraterrestrial races on Viera or bring their biospheres near a planet during interventions. (the best known is *The Black Arrow* seen in Nuremberg in 1561 which was none other than Viera Andromeda).

• The Arcturians - Dieslientiplex •
Boötes Constellation – Planet Pitolla

. Language: Nxataexeratae – telepathic only. They prefer not to emit sounds and only use telepathy.

. Physical appearance: 1,10-1,30m, devoid of hair system, resemble *Small Greys*, but with turquoise skin covered in places, of warts in broad purple patches, dolphin head with an ear-to-ear mouth, cat eyes, no ears, no nose, 3 fingers/toes. Feed by liquid chemicals absorbed mainly through their skin.

. Temperament: loving, very emotional, symbolists, lovers of great technological advances.

. Objectives: one of the oldest races that have shaped the Earth, involved since the beginning of its evolution and on which they implanted the first protohuman races of hominins and brought the first groups of animals with the help of the Etorthans (Orion, Rigel). Share their wisdom and technological advances.

• The Ummites (Oomans) •
Originating from Wolf424, planet Ummo (Oomo) and Ooeaaks

. Language: they use a planetary language and on Earth a written method of communication which they define as a neurolinguistic structure adapted to the current culture, which, according to them, reflects theirs only partially and not chronologically.

The vast majority of Ummites are devoid of vocal cords; They mainly use telepathy. They have technologies that can not only read thoughts, but project them before they come to fruition.

. Land bases: 150 expeditionary personnel work there -

as of September 1st, 2021, there are 66 in Europe, 30 in North America, 30 in South America, 12 in Asia, and 12 in Antarctica.

The neurolinguistic system was analyzed by linguist Jean Pollion in *UMMO, real aliens!* [66], and some of their scientific concepts, by the astrophysicist Jean-Pierre Petit in *Cosmic Contacts. The aliens are among us! How far can one think too far?* co-written with Jean-Claude Bourret [64]:

« We call BUUALEEXII the coherent and conscious in-formational body that the BUUAWOEMII (synergistic tandem soul/organism) feeds into the BUUAWAAE BIIAEIIEE (collective consciousness) during its coupling. The BUUALEEXII contains all the data on intercosmo-biological animation corresponding to the existence of an OEMII (human), it is somehow its double in BUUA-WAAE BIIAEIIEE. When the OEMII (body) dies and the chain of atoms DIIUYAA (krypton) that constitutes the OEMBUUAW (connectic structure) is completely bro-ken, the BUUALEEXII then retains its links with the BUUAWA (soul) through the UELIBUUAW OAAE (seat of the primary consciousness of BUUAWA) which is also located in the BUUAWAAE BIIAEIIEE. [3] »

. Physical appearance: 1.60-2.00m, Nordic Swedish-style, skin of different tones, round eyes and iris of different colors, 5 fingers/toes. Omnivorous.

. Temperament: autonomous at a very early age, they leave their parents and are educated very strictly in specialized centers, then selected, according to their skills to serve their communities. They appreciate low temperatures can read with their fingertips and the soles of their feet. Their society is managed by a planetary artificial intelligence called *Xanmo Ayubaa*. They love to create *perfume concerts.*

. Objectives: scientific minds endowed with a rigorous and methodical logic, their uncompromising words invite us to question our society and its destructive tendencies. They help to protect the planet, develop a tetravalent perspective of the cosmic reality, share new concepts and technical information for the evolution of sciences, train Earthlings with new scientific paradigms, and encourage the reform of Earth educational systems.

• The Taygetan - Pleiadians •
Taurus Constellation, TauriAA, Planets, Erra, Temmer, Procyon and Dakote

. Language: similar to Hebrew + major earthly languages + telepathy.

. Physical appearance: 1.50m-2.20m, usually called *Nordics* or *Blonds* in ufological literature, they have different skin tones, round eyes and iris of different colors, 5 fingers/toes. Vegans. Matriarchal societies run by women (75% female – 25% male undernumbered).

. Temperament: groups of women, loving, come especially to help, strategic and powerful, concerned by the excesses of Earth Elites.

. Objectives: they are very active and had 20 ships and 25,000 crew members in 2016-2018 under the responsibility of Five Star General Asket of Temmer (contact of Swiss Eduard Albert, *aka* Billy Meier) [54], but have only one left in 2021, managed by 35 crew members ; a few are communicating with Earth contactees. They have taken on the role of *whistleblowers* and inform

Earth's populations of the reality of extraterrestrials, and of interlinked diplomatic relations and off-planet interferences.

• The P'ntl Zetas •
Constellation Zeta Reticuli II, binary star,
5th planet called P'ntl *(pronounce: pon-tal)*

. Language: *Rapid* murmur, difficult to grasp at first + English + 100% telepathic accompanied by gestural or facial expressions. (have vocal cords and can speak, but prefer the telepathic way they teach on social networks):

- kwh *(Ki-Wah-Hou)*: Earthlings (*Blue Water Peoples*)
- cjcj whh (*Djai-Djai-Wah-Ha*): what's up? OK?
- K'k' (*kii-kii*): thank you.

. Physical appearance: 1.37m, nocturnal humans, without hair system, resemble *Small Greys*, but are very different; gray skin, large round eyes of different colors, two eyelids, night vision in color, small nose, teeth, but no ears, 4 fingers/toes. Ancient semi-aquatic genotype, they can breathe underwater. Pesco vegetarians, they like to savour the varieties of coffees from exceptional terroirs. Friends of the Sasquatch (Big Foot).

. Temperament: neutral nation, very loving and caring, peaceful, love humor, love-joy, consider children sacred, and enjoy extreme sports.

. Objectives: they are implanted on Earth in underground bases not connected to those of the Reptilian-Draconians, a vast information complex that they restore, located at the top of Sandia Mountains near Albuquerque in the USA. The station is 3 km deep and occupies an old abandoned tunnel system where they have been living for 15,000 years.
They manage 8 information stations: 4 terrestrial and 4 underwater.

Very involved in the OFC | Official First Contact | they share their *Light*, Earth History, the teaching of telepathy, archaeoplanetography and who they are, pushing the boundaries of preconceived ideas, especially for what it means to be human. They consider it impolite to group together the stellar nations that are different worlds, each with a culture, a History, and unique beliefs as if they formed only one set called the *Small Greys* and that it is detrimental to see only the color of an individual's skin instead of the person. [83]

• The Sirians •
From Sirius A and C, planet Xylanthia.

. Language: articulated + main Earth languages + 100% telepathy (some groups use consonantal clicks (see description in previous paragraph *Typologies of languages and dialects).*

. Physical appearance: 1,60-1,90m, Nordic, large cat eyes of different colors, purple-blue skin, can switch colors according to their emotions or the environment (like chameleons); some Sirian peoples have gills and can evolve either on land or underwater, webbed fingers/toes, frugivores or vegans.

. Temperament: they like proximity and very large families of 30-40 people in which all members feel close. Calm, very friendly, attentive and joyful like dolphins, which are also of Sirian origin.

. Objectives: they have very advanced technologies and work with Earthlings on the concepts of space-time and timelines. They help to develop an ecological system adapted to human evolution, by improving the biological and magnetic energy grid of the planet, by protecting the environment and biodiversity, and by raising Earth's consciousness.

ART. 8 – Emotional Communication
Do extraterrestrials affect our emotions?

Emotions are strongly repressed on Earth as if it were something inappropriate that must be suppressed, especially by the members of the male population. If a man cries in your presence, his behavior is considered inappropriate and people who cry in front of a camera, during an interview, repress their tears at all costs and apologize.

On Earth, detachment has acquired capital importance on many philosophical, religious and psychoanalytic levels. In the History of Ancient Philosophy, *Nicolas Laforêt* [47] presents the original stoic perspective of Marcus Aurelius «the detachment of the world...of all things...of riches, pleasures and honors.» The Stoic ethic invites man to take a distance without being inactive, idle or indifferent.

The notion of detachment or non-attachment is also at the heart of religions, in Christianity, Hinduism, Jainism, Sufism or Taoism which presents it as an indispensable prerequisite to the process of ultimate liberation, enlightenment. In Buddhist philosophy, Upādāna (appropriation or attachment) can be associated with sensorial thirst, misconceptions, rituals or personality. The practice of meditation techniques makes it possible to take a step back and detach oneself mentally and emotionally in order to develop a neutral attitude or the Middle Way.

The blue gods of Asia were Andromedans. They lived on this part of the planet thousands of years ago. They are the ones who implemented the original forms of Buddhism and Hinduism and consequently the notion of non-attachment.

The Andromedans and the oldest interstellar races practice spiritual *non-attachment, the inner state of a person unaffected by the situations of daily existence. They* consider emotional complacency, lack of maturity and wisdom, and emotional races, not yet accomplished or not yet realized. In the Great Stellar Councils, it is the non-emotional, logical and rational races that have the most weight in decision-making, to the detriment of the younger, emotional or ultra-emotional races.

On Earth, the best thing is to find the right balance. Some people have more emotions than others. You may choose those that seem appropriate to you and reject those that seem inappropriate to you. You can select and control them. There's a big difference between *mastering* your emotions and *controlling* your emotions. It is about mastery. It's not about self-control.

Until you clearly understand what these two terms imply, it will be difficult for you to master your life, as you will try to do so through control. Similarly, as long as you believe that self-mastering is a way of control, you will persist in trying to control yourself or everything around you. But it is precisely by stopping the control that mastery develops.

. Control — is based on fear. It is strategic and requires constant energy expenditure to be maintained. When you try to control something or someone, you really mean you don't control them.

. Mastery — is based on trust, relaxation, acceptance. It is an art based on a thorough knowledge of self and life.

You can develop a deep feeling of the fundamental differences between *mastery* and *control*, by practicing meditation and realizing that you are already the master of your life because life is a constantly living and uncontrollable dynamic and what prevents you from realizing it is ... control!

ART. 9 – Energy communication
Why do I have tinnitus or wheezing in my ears or in my lower skull?

Millions of people in Europe, the USA and Japan in particular hear tinnitus. These are auditory sensations perceptible by a person and inaudible to his entourage. The sound may resemble whistling, humming, ringing, rattling, musical notes or sounds heard in the ears or felt in the bones of the skull. They can be unilateral on one side of the head, bilateral on both sides, or on the back of the head, at the base of the skull. The intensity is variable: high or low, the tone is very acute, low or very low and slow or fast, uniform or pulsed and they can occur very regularly at specific times.

Sounds may appear to come from within the body or from outside, and may be permanent, intermittent, variable, or temporary.

If you are in good health and without any particular problems, from a stellar point of view, these hum can be due to vibrational waves or signals transmitted by the crews of your stellar family, raising your frequencies from their spacecrafts.

From Earth scientific research, tinnitus is a warning symptom of hearing impairment and can affect the quality of life. It is therefore very important, if you have any, to rest, to meditate in soothing and quiet places, and especially to consult an otolaryngologist (ENT) doctor or an osteopath who will make a medical diagnosis and find appropriate solutions after reviewing the organic, mechanical or physiological causes.

The hypotheses about their origins are the dysfunction of the auditory system following a state of generalized physical or intellectual fatigue, occupational stress, auditory or cranial trauma, the taking of ototoxic drugs, or different types of infections.

The stellar aspect of tinnitus is discussed in the following paragraph.

ART. 10 – Communication using dreams
Are dreams used by extraterrestrials as communication tools? Do we go into other real realities when we dream?

Stellars use your sleep phases to convey dreamlike messages. They use two preferred modes:

.natural mode - spontaneous and intuitive natural telepathy or

.artificial mode - advanced technologies of arrangement and trans-formation of frequencies, and we receive them during the day, as waking dreams, intuitions, realizations or premonitions, and du-ring the night, as dreams or nightmares.

The duration of stellar days varies according to their lineages. Some are spread over 60 hours; they are long waking days for them, during which you will sleep at least two nights; They will use communication techniques that will influence you as they are awake while you are asleep and reception is easier during sleep phases.

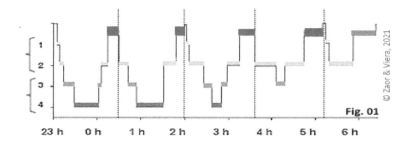

Fig. 01

Sleep is a very active psychological phenomenon involving many neurological processes and cerebral wave phases that extraterrestrials take advantage of; Dreamlike activity is most intense during the REM sleep phase.

Sleep plays an important role in the processing of the information we receive or transmit throughout the day and it has an impact on the management, storage and cleansing of the superfluous information, emotions or memories.

1. Slow Wave Sleep

The first step of your night: slow and quiet wave sleep is very active! The majority of your sleep time is devoted to slow-wave sleep, since it occupies 80% of our sleep time. It consists of four phases:

-Stage I: a few minutes – 8-14 Hz Alpha waves
you find yourself in a state of near unconsciousness, you you wake up easily and if asked a question, you give vague answers.

-Stage II: 30-45 min – 4-8 Hz Theta waves
light sleep during which you can still wake up easily.

-Stage III: 30 min semi-deep - Delta waves from 0.5 to 4 Hz

the waves amplify; emergence of deep sleep, lengthening

of the dream phase. It will be harder to wake you up.

-Stage IV: 30 min deep – 0.5 to 4 Hz delta waves

the electric waves emitted by your brain are very large.

You are in a very deep sleep and you cannot be awakened

easily.

2. Fast Wave 'REM' Sleep

2nd stage of your night: 1h30 after falling asleep

for 10 min – 20 to 45 Hz Gamma waves.

During REM sleep, brain waves accelerate abruptly, your

neck relaxes, your eyes move in all directions, your body

and your breathing become jerky. Your brain is truly energi-

zed and "blows up" your internal circuit breaker - that's

when you start dreaming for ten minutes.

3. Organization of sleep cycles

then a new full cycle begins: slow-wave sleep followed by

fast-wave sleep and these four phases of sleep will repeat

on average 4 to 6 times a night, until you wake up.

The dream is a disposition of the mind that allows the individual to free himself from chronological Earth time and space, and to access the supernatural, the divine and can be used as a therapeutic means, of knowledge or of revelation.

Philosophical, psychological, psychodynamic or neurobiological scientific approaches make it a process anchored in physicality related to brain activity. But in general, we dream all the time, not just during the sleep period; we also dream during the day and it is then possible to perceive what is beyond the known, beyond the sensory spectra: etheric or astral frequencies.

4. Lucid dreams and rested aliveness

Dream, waking dream, altered states of consciousness or meditation allow two or more different converging timelines to live simultaneously. These conditions develop when the brain releases gamma waves.

Meditation in particular has the ability to generate a state of consciousness of *rested aliveness* that produces a more ordered physiological state, the relaxation of tensions, and an increase in intelligence and creativity as well as key moments of discovery and spontaneous realization during gamma wave peaks.

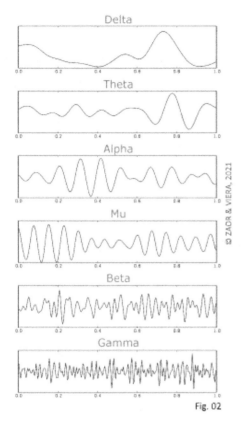

Fig. 02

You can use your imagination as a focus of attention and meditate. Do not only practice meditation as a relaxation exercise, but as a tool for deepening oneself. This exercise will turn into lucid dreams, then out of body (OBE) and finally into the acceptance of a new reality. Your physicality has limits, but not your imagination or your creativity.

When you dream, you are these density because you create them to experience them. Whatever you feel and think, whatever the levels of your vibrations or frequencies, intent or concentration, this reality manifests itself immediately. But it can remain latent and will only manifest more clearly during your sleep. You can have fun doing tests. Here again, the key is meditation and the keeping of a *dream journal* that can be used as a basis for personal questioning and deepening.

Moreover, the conscious/subconscious/supraconscious divisions are the binary and dual limitations of reality which, in itself, is not dual and cannot be divided. Transcendent sensibility can grasp the universal principles or mechanics directly only if it is itself of a universal order.

ART. 11 – Extrasensory communication (ESP)
Is the intuition connected to an extraterrestrial connection?

The intuition, from the Latin *presæ-, before* and *dicere, say*: before (let the perception be put into words), is defined by the National Centre for Textual and Lexical Resources [18]:

1. a direct understanding

« to discover, to guess, to predict, to anticipate, to feel, someone or something at the outset, without going through the stages of analysis, reasoning or reflection. »

From a philosophical point of view, it is:

2. a clear evidence

« a truth that appears to the mind with clarity...a direct, fundamental, first, pure intuition. »

René Guénon, in *La Métaphysique Orientale* [32] marks the difference between:

3. intellectual intuition and 4. perceptual intuition

« Science is discursive rational knowledge, always indirect, knowledge by reflection; metaphysics is supra-rational, intuitive and immediate knowledge.

Moreover, this pure intellectual intuition, without which there is no true metaphysics, must in no way be assimilated to the intuition of which some contemporary philosophers speak, for it is, on the contrary, infrarational. There is an intellectual intuition and a sensitive intuition. »

11.1 – Extrasensory Perceptions - ESP

Alan Turing, British mathematician and cryptologist, author of works that lay the scientific foundations of computer science, points out that:

« [the] extrasensory perception...namely telepathy, clairvoyance, precognition and psychokinesis...[are] disturbing phenomena [that] seem to deny all our usual scientific ideas.

How we would like to discredit them!

Unfortunately, the statistical evidence, at least for telepathy, is overwhelming. It's very difficult to reorganize your ideas to incorporate these new facts. Once we accept them, it's no longer very useful to believe in ghosts...

The idea that our bodies simply move according to the known laws of physics, as well as others not yet discovered but somewhat similar, would be one of the first to disappear. [81] »

11.2 – ESP and stellar (extraterrestrial) telepathy

Stellars (extraterrestrials) say that intuition, telepathy, ESP and intuitive communication are not limited to the brain, but are:

a) a common pole, a universal egregore, *accumulator-generator* of information,

(b) multiple versions of each of us, living at the same time, in a multitude of other realities that occupy the same space that we occupy, that are here and not here at the same time,

71

(c) artificial technological influences,

(d) intuitive extraterrestrial influences or communications.

In other words, given that time does not exist linearly or chronologically - past, present, future - and that everything is here and now and all at once, intuitive people have developed the ability to be in direct communication with these different sources, to draw on the information they need.

ART. 12 – Telepathic Communication
Is Earth telepathy credible? What is the difference between Earth telepathy and stellar (extraterrestrial) telepathy?

Telepathy refers to the exchange of information, thoughts, places, images, feelings, felt, between two or more people not involving any sensory interaction. It is not recognized by conventional science, but it is widely used in science fiction and in alternative sciences, self-development or ufology.

In parapsychology, telepathy is part of extrasensory perceptions, as a precursor to precognition and clairvoyance, the ability to know events, acquired otherwise than by logical deduction and the ability to extract feelings or information that would somehow infiltrate into you, beyond the known.

The term was coined by physicists Gurney *et al.* in 1882 in *Phantasms of the Living*, translated by M. Marillier, *Telepathic Hallucinations* [33]:

> « The phenomena which may give us some reason to suppose that the spirit of one man has acted upon the spirit of another, without one having uttered a word, or written a word, or made a sign. We have given .. the name telepathy to this transmission of thoughts or feelings...and ranked among the telepathic phenomena a

vast class of facts that seem, at first glance, very different from a simple transmission of thought. »

According to Myers *et al.* « It was in the magnetic state that we observed for the first time the transmission of thought...a certain community of sensations between the operator and the subject ... (magnetism [described as] the ability to transmit restricted thought for the operator to the subject alone, and made more intense by it). »

Many stellars (extraterrestrials) are only telepathic and no longer use articulated languages, neither written nor spoken. They are 100% telepathic and must develop methods to protect their thoughts, feelings or privacy that would otherwise be completely accessible to their peers.

Other lineages can be both telepathic and use articulated languages. So not all interstellar lineages can communicate with Earthlings due to lack of common means of communication.

They assert that natural or artificial telepathy, synthetic or psychotronic telepathy technologies, techlepathy, will become inevitable for the future on Earth and in the development of our relations with them. They point out that telepathy is a natural ability that Earthlings have lost at birth due to the bridging of Earth frequencies by advanced technologies from the Moon-Biosphere and Earth education that does not include these capabilities [84].

All that lives beyond the Earth's magnetosphere is in 50 Hz and the individual capacities or groups of telepathic, clairvoyant or clairaudient percipients, are much more developed than on Earth. Earthlings must practice them, rework them to develop them.

ART. 13 – Inspirational communication
Do Extraterrestrials use the arts and artistic creation to inspire us and send messages? Does the music contain programs that act on our mind without our knowledge? Does classical music stimulate the brain?

Stellars (extraterrestrials) use this mode of interaction almost all the time! They call it *intuitive telepathy*. When you receive it, you feel inspired and guided by a creative force.

They often desynchronize your body frequency from that of your environment, which increases your personal frequency and a re-synchronization takes place closer to 50 Hz.

You may have many waking dreams, or feel like you no longer belong to Earth, or to the systems that govern it. And it increases your desire to find yourself at home, on your home planet.

Music affects brain waves in different ways and not all types of music have the same significant impact, however, once exposed to the sound frequencies of classical music, the measurement of mental performance can be significantly improved.

Music can be programmed to affect the human mind both positively and negatively.

From a positive point of view: the binaural beat or its binaural at 432 Hz is an auditory artifact, an apparent sound perception emerging in the brain by specific physical stimuli which will put you in a pre-meditative state.

The same applies to music raising frequencies to 963 Hz.

From a negative point of view: some classical or modern musiccan be dark and invite low frequencies and emotions of the same type. Some songs do it more than others.

ART. 14 – The awakening of consciousness and psychotropics
Is the use of natural or artificial psychotropics recommended for spiritual awakening or to open oneself to the cosmic reality?

According to the early studies of the academician, psychiatrist, neurologist and brilliant writer Jean Delay who wrote *Brain Waves and Psychology* in 1942, « a psychotropic is a chemical product or substance that induces a psychological tropism and acts mainly on the state of the central nervous system by modifying certain bio-chemical and physiological processes of the brain. By altering brain functions, a psychotropic induces change in perception, sensations, mood, consciousness (altered states of consciousness) or other psychological or behavioral functions. »

The work of R. Schultes [70] and W. La Barre [46], mentions that the use of psychotropic plants is essential in the ideology and religious practice on the entire surface of the planet; the extreme seniority of their use is determined by their uniformity of practice which would testify to an unconscious structuring, culturally programmed to accept the ecstatic experience within the framework of an organized cult. Thus, the Paleolithic hunters who arrived in America were culturally predisposed to collect and prepare psychotropic plants.

A high percentage of the Earth's population uses natural or artificial psychotropic drugs to overcome self-imposed or self-inflicted limits:

78

- alcohol and tobacco are stimulants,

- neuroleptics are sedative,

- hallucinogens or psychedelics are dissociative,

Chronological and linear time is the deliberate result of the illusion created by humanity in 3rd density. Psychotropics break these concepts and propel an artificial awareness that must be renewed in a natural way through meditation because the learning experience is a 3-D immersive sensory process that is used to discover who we are, to let go of what needs to be, to create synergy with ourselves and what surrounds us in order to *accomplish* oneself, or be *realized*.

ART. 15 – Intuitive communication
An example of intuitive communication between an Earthling and two extraterrestrials in a military context

In his book, *ABOVE BLACK, Sergeant Dan* Sherman documents his professional experience in an intuitive communication program developed by the US government, directly in contact with two extraterrestrials [72].

U.S. Air Force Sergeant (USAF) at the United States National Security Agency (NSA), Sherman joined the United States Air Force like most other Americans, very proud to serve his country and his military training. During his twelve years of service, he was recognized for his heroism, received several medals of honor and was honored for his actions in the War in the Persian Gulf.

He was 24 at the time of the incident. He began training as an electronic intelligence analyst, ELINT (EL: Electronic – INT: Intelligence), where he learned to analyze the internal characteristics of energy emanating from equipment, such as radars, to determine the type of transmissions and for what purpose the equipment was being used.

But in parallel, his superiors offered him to follow another training, the first one serving as a cover for the second: the PPD *Project Preserve Destiny* a secret government project that would radically change his life.

His world will turn upside down, when the captain tells him that random tests had been conducted to determine the genetic compatibility of a part of the population and his mother had been visited by extraterrestrials in the summer of 1960. While he was still a fetus in her womb, they *implanted* him and *genetically manipulated* him to have special abilities and be able to *speak* with them through *intuitive communications*. And without any further ado, he also revealed that the American government had been in contact with extraterrestrials since 1947.

Needless to say, Sherman was shocked.

Before continuing this story, please link several dates and information:

1. 1947: Roswell crash and first official testimony of Kenneth Albert Arnold, pilot under license no. 333487, who was conducting an aerial survey with his plane near Mount Rainier, Washington, USA, and who noticed nine mysterious objects flying at twice the speed of sound [84],

2. 1936...1947 and 1954: treaties and agreements signed between different world governments and various extraterrestrial lineages (ART. 19 & 20),

3. 1954 : Elizabeth Klarer's intercourse with Centaurian Akon from Planet Meton and their offspring named Ayling (ART.

31),

4. 1957 : abduction and incourse between Brazilian Antonio Villas-Boas and a human type extraterrestrial female (ART. 31),

5. 1960: start of the Preserve Destiny Project which became operational in 1963 and ended in 1968 – in 1961: first widely mediated story of a kidnapping by Zeta Reticuli: Betty and Barney Hill [84],

6. Reports of abductions, hybridization, training and psychic power development, in the presence of stellars (extraterrestrials) often *Tall Grays* and *Small Greys* accompanied by soldiers, are increasingly reported, especially during sessions of regressive hypnosis [52.40]

So stellars (extraterrestrials) are present, they have been spotted by the population, agreements and treaties have been signed with different heads of governments, extraterrestrials are now living and working in underground bases, random tests are carried out to determine genetic compatibility, and nominal lists have been drawn...abductions of humans and animals are in full swing.

But Sergeant Sherman doesn't know any of this. He is 24 years old, he came for training in the hope of developing a military career...and his captain, standing before him in a very calm and relaxed way, shares this explosive information as if it were a rumor that he had read in a newspaper the day before, and says:

« I know it's hard to swallow, but I can assure you it's true. »

Sherman wondered if he wasn't dreaming...he had heard about tests on new extraterrestrial technologies in Nevada...but now, it was no longer a rumor...it had suddenly become his reality.

His captain then specified what he meant by *unique abilities:*

« — Your capabilities are the product of the DPP. These are skills that allow you to communicate through the intuitive manipulation of your mind. Within the military, a handful of employees have already perfected them and used them.

Many other people in the world population have these abilities, but until they are activated and developed by appropriate exercises, they will remain dormant.

...

The first embryo that was a genetic success and developed under the supervision of the PPD program was produced for the first time in January 1963. There are only a small number of NSA employees who can communicate intuitively, hence the waiting phase. These abilities cannot be fully utilized until subjects reach 25 years of age. The program ended in March 1968. [72] »

His first lesson, in the PPD course, was to listen to a tone, to look on a screen where boxes had different types of sinusoidal waves; he had to memorize a first tone, hum it mentally (not verbally), find out which wave it was and try to flatten it. He did it with one wave, then 2, then 3 ... up to 10. Over time, he will have a first conversation with an extraterrestrial, then after being transferred to another base, with a second.

But during the second set of communications he will realize that the extraterrestrial transmits the coordinates of abductions... and that this is obviously happening in a military context. He then decided to leave the army.

He will then understand that his professional choices were directed by the extraterrestrials or by the army, so that he would end up where he was at the moment and to activate his skills to communicate with extraterrestrials.

The stellars (extraterrestrials) and the Zeta Reticuli or *Small Greys* mentioned in this program have no vocal cords and are only tele-pathic. They communicate in this immersive way with the Earth-lings who are capable of receiving it, sometimes enveloping them in an immersive electromagnetic bubble. It is beyond telepathy, because the person can receive the messages not only mentally, but also *feel* them with all senses and physically with the body. They are *felt in the flesh*, as cold is felt by the skin, or moisture by the bones.

ART. 16 – Smart technologies
What technologies induce telepathy artificially?

It is difficult to discern it — as one must sweep wide, over a long period and a slow deployment over the centuries — but an imperceptible and radical transformation of society seems to be moving towards two trends. Some do not know that this movement is fomented by interstellar races, promote the change or on the contrary, resist and hinder it. In either case without being aware of it, they follow the development program of Earth humanity under extraterrestrial control.

At first glance, these changes that take place over a period of several decades, even centuries, seem to be parts of people's development and the result of a natural evolution. But when looking more closely, they seem to be increasingly based on artificial structures that feed the power and control systems.

Those who do not know that extraterrestrial groups are involved in the treaty-validated development of humanity, believe that small groups of elites are responsible for these changes... they may, but they are not the initiators. They respond to extraterrestrial incentives and influences and are also subject to manipulation that they pass on to the populations. Their responsibility lies in the fact that they agree to do so.

One might indeed wonder why military organizations supported or controlled by transnational corporations would spend an unlimited amount of resources, effort and time to consolidate their control of the planet? Why do they pursue an objective that they themselves, under cover of secrecy, deem destructive?

The answer is simple: they are controlled by extraterrestrials whose purposes depend on the races that set them up: to help earthly humanity or to keep this control and acquire it by force.

16.1 – Types of Technologies

You may have noticed that at the prow of all kinds of pro- or anti-movements, intelligent technologies initiate, structure and control societal waves that knead humanities.

Among the tools and technologies used are:

. Planetary networks of man-machine artificial intelligence and nation, group or individual targeting technologies;
. Artificial telepathy tools, thought reading and subliminal messaging for neurolinguistic programming;
. Remote neuronal monitoring, used to measure its effects;
. The incorporation of implants for behavioral change;
. Cellular towers and transmitting of specific frequencies and messages;

. Drones and satellites to do this from space on much larger areas or, conversely, *surgically* targeted;

Developing these technologies in detail could be the subject of a book. I will limit my sharing to an experience with my contacts in which natural telepathy (theirs and mine) and artificial telepathy were combined. In the previous ART. 6, I mentioned:

« The synchronicity of events seemed to be done artificially, calculated and perfectly organized. It was just amazing. I have discovered over time that Zen or other stellars possess advanced technologies that allow organizing or reorganize events in a person's life.

The first interstellar lineage that contacted me, in March 2016, tested many aspects of my personality, my knowledge, my integrity or spirituality over several months, and they shared advanced technologies using me as a test subject so I would know what the effects were. »

16.2 – Example of a practical application of an extraterrestrial technology

They would test me without ever telling me what they were doing; I had to find out on my own. This time it was rather surprising: they could see what I was seeing, using my eyes.

Many tests had been done in the past with people who had been abducted and had had eye implants. These objects looked like contact lenses; they had a ceramic exterior and the interior contained different types of technologies unknown at the time.

In my case, there were no implants. I began to realize I was not alone in looking at something. Someone else was seeing it at the same time and was using my eyes to look at what I was seeing. It's a rather weird feeling to realize that someone else was using my eyes...and the good joke they were playing at me !

I told Zen about it, and he confirmed this was going on. They then decided to show me how they use it. We disconnected and they sent me a telepathic message telling me to go to a small town in Southern France. During the journey, I was alone to see, but as soon as I arrived I felt that they connected to my eyes and that they were watching what I was watching. Telepathically, I told them that I was going to look at the specific places they were going to point me to and that we would discuss it later.

They first sent me to a small store where there was a vertical display stand on which bracelets with names were stacked...when I read the names, I saw that there were three grouped one just above the other and the names (shortened and Frenchified) were from three of my contacts.

They then sent me to another store where magnificent crystals were displayed. I looked at one of them, made a connection between the crystal and one of my contacts and asked if they found it beautiful.

They sent me to a large park and asked me if I could see the discoidal ship stationed there. But I couldn't see anything.

16.3 – The Knight in the Red Cape

I continued to wander through the narrow streets of this medieval city and I saw before me a mother with a young seven-year-old boy, who was jumping around having fun. He wore a knight's disguise, a red cape with a large black Occitan cross, and a black sword in his right hand.

I thought I would check if I could have control over their technology.

I stopped my thoughts and completely drained my brain off thoughts and intentionally and quickly turned my gaze to something else to see if they would notice.

During the debriefing the next day, they told me: 1. they had placed the bracelets in this order so that I could see them and realize their abilities - 2. the crystal chosen was the birthstone of the extraterrestrial to whom I had linked it to - 3. I had not seen the ship because it was in invisible mode - and finally they were very sorry...but I had not received the telepathic message to observe the young boy in the red cape and I had not seen him! ...to my delight, I was rather amused to tell them that I had intentionally fooled them ... they were surprised and burst out laughing!

16.4 – How to disable artificial telepathy

While letting them experiment their technologies on me, I also became aware, at the same time, that it is possible to change the technology frequencies or impact on me.

It is what they have to do when they want to disconnect from the control of their artificial intelligence. Here is an excerpt from the book *ARTIFICIAL (1.4 STELLAR TAKEOFF)*

« The ZU1 is long and tapered like the tip of an arrow. It is 100 m long and 30 m wide. It is managed by ZIA its artificial intelligence which is entirely and specifically dedicated to it and which is the very extension of Capt. Ellis... When Capt. Ellis thinks something, Zia thinks it simultaneously. And vice versa. [84] »

Stellars (extraterrestrials) are connected 24/24 hours to each other thanks not only to their natural telepathy, but also to the artificial intelligence that manage their daily lives. There is no crime in their societies, because as soon as someone in their world, or an individual of another race has threatening intentions...everyone knows it immediately. They don't have to try to communicate with each other, but they have to disconnect from the two systems when they want to have private thoughts. On Earth we learn to connect telepathically, but they learn to disconnect to protect their thoughts.

These technologies are used by ill-intentioned races to control Earth populations, or on the contrary by a well-intentioned race to limit the actions of a person that can be dangerous for all.

But they can also be used with people who want to learn, increase their frequencies and enter into telepathic communication.

Chapter 2

EXOPOLITICS AND EXODIPLOMACY

ART. 17 – Extraterrestrial Perspectives, First Directive and Federation structures
How do stellars (extraterrestrials) perceive Earthlings?

17.1 – Extraterrestrial perspectives

The stellars (extraterrestrials) do not apprehend Earth human being, under the only anthropological viewpoint, physical, anatomical, biological, morphological, physiological, evolutionary, or only and simply cultural: social, religious, linguistic, psychological, geographical, but, they take into account each individual as such, as a combined system, connected and associated with larger, local, planetary or cosmic, undivided sets.

Each person is perceived as a biological *garment*, artificially standardized at low frequency, adapted and synchronized for a stellar (extraterrestrial) who would make the choice, *put it on* or *slip into it* for one reason: to experience being a human living on Earth.

They study it from two angles:

- the natural aspect of a *soul* which they will follow in its evolutionary totality through multiple incarnations on different planets and within different races, or

- artificial: the development of a body associated with the artificial intelligence that makes it work.

17.2 – The Prime Directive

The Homo sapiens on earth has progressed dramatically since the industrial era of the last 250 years, but he is unfortunately still considered fiery, dangerous and violent; an archaic, often aggressive, colonizing species not yet developed in terms of societal structures, devoid of rationality, with a low level of intelligence and a serious lack of consciousness and spirituality; a statement written in the articles of the Prime Directive [84] which governs their relations with indigenous peoples – the text of the Prime Directive was communicated to me on 27 February 2017.

PRIME DIRECTIVE

Andromeda High Council

within

the United Federation of Planets

Chapter VI, Article II, Paragraph VII

I

The Prime Directive serves as a moral, ethical and legal guide. It takes precedence over all other considerations and carries the highest moral obligation.

II

The most solemn oath of a ship's captain is to give his life, or even that of his crew, rather than violate the Prime Directive.

III

The Prime Directive is applicable to all cultures on a planet that has not yet reached interstellar travel capacity and have not established an organized continuous relationship with an evolved interstellar culture.

IV

No article of the Prime Directive authorizes the staff of the Andromeda High Council within the United Federation of Planets to intervene in matters which are essentially within the domestic, local or private jurisdiction of any planetary system, or submit the members to the regulations of the articles

of the Andromeda High Council within the United Federation
of Planets.

V

As the right of every sensitive species to live according to the
universal law of free will in accordance with its natural and
biological cultural evolution is considered sacred, no member
or staff of the Andromeda High Council within the United Federation of Planets may interfere with the normal, autonomous and healthy functioning of the development of indigenous life, society and culture. Such interference includes the
introduction of knowledge, or superior technologies, into a
world whose members and society are unable to manage
these benefits wisely, and which are assessed by their
present level of spiritual, moral, and technological evolution.

VI

The personnel of the Andromeda High Council within the United Federation of Planets shall not be permitted to come into
contact with non-interstellar races or developing races, by
any technological means, used or in service now or to invent
in the future, unless the said race is threatened by an external source.

VII

Should it occur that an external source, hostile or unfriendly,
threatens the normal development of the said non-interstel-

lar race in question, the personnel of the Andromeda High Council within the United Federation of Planets, may contact members of such a race only using their own technological apparatus and means of communication already used by that race. No communication device currently in use, or to be invented in the future, can be of a higher technological level than that of the race. Spiritual or ethical knowledge is also limited to the bare minimum necessary, and using only methods and devices of communication at the current level of understanding of the contacted race.

VIII

If face-to-face personal contact is required, it shall be kept to a minimum and when a member of the staff of the Andromeda High Council within the United Federation of Planets is designated for such contact, he or she must have the closest physical appearance and resemblance to the race in question. To the extent possible, the dress protocol of the race that is being contacted must be respected and used.

IX

It is forbidden to communicate to any resident native of this planet, any device, machine, tool, weapon or invention representing an improvement of the science and technology already existing on this planet unless this need is previously analyzed and approved by the Andromeda High Council within the

United Federation of Planets and it must be done with the intention of promoting a controlled improvement in the quality of life of the race being contacted.

X

Nothing in the articles of the Prime Directive authorizes the staff of the Andromeda High Council within the United Federation of Planets to intervene on matters which are essentially within the national jurisdiction of any planetary social system, and does not require members to make regulations under these sections. But this principle does not prejudice the application of the implementing measures provided for in Chapter VI.

Stellars (extraterrestrials) consider that a species is *less evolved* as long as it has not developed its interstellar space capabilities. This status is achieved thanks to the development of means of transport (such as spacecraft or man-made biospheres), and advanced technologies, zero-point energy, the abandonment of ionizing nuclear energy, and above all the spiritual and ethical maturity of the peoples capable of evolving in space autonomously, as one and the same whole.

17.3 – Federations, Councils and Alliances

On January 9, 2020, I spoke with my contacts about the various organizations that manage galactic zones and the relations with Earth. There are a lot of them and it would be impossible to list them all. Here is what they said:

- the terms *Confederation, Galactic Confederation, Galactic Federation, Galactic Federation of Worlds* are terms used by Earth organizations. No interstellar civilization originating from outside planet Earth and from other solar systems, refers to the galaxy.

The UFoP, the United Federation of Planets, does not manage or monitor the entire galaxy and there is no confederation or consortium above it. The Milky Way is huge and consists of billions upon billions of civilizations. It is practically impossible for a single body, no matter how powerful, to manage such a gigantic system.

UFoP operates only in this quadrant of the galaxy (divided into four). The federation represents only a few thousand civilizations and it is so important that it already represents a difficulty in itself, to manage them all.

Some Alliances are called:

- *The Alliance of the Spheres* or *Alliance of the Blue Spheres:* this is the best known; it is composed of the Andromedans, the Arcturian-Dieslientiplex and the Blue Avians,
- the *Council of Nine* (these are extraterrestrial races and not secret groups on Earth),
- the *Ohallu Council,*
- the *High Council of Arcturian-Dieslientiplex-Devonians-Ko-rendians,*
- the *Feline Alliance,*
- the *Agarthian-Telosian Council,*
- the *High Council of Alcyone,*

...

In general there is an incalculable number of Alliances and Councils because each space zone, each solar system and each planet has its own alliances, High Councils, and Planetary or Community Councils; none is hierarchically above the UFoP.

ART. 18 – Contact with Earth
Have extraterrestrials made contact with world governments? Why is there so much secrecy about their existence?

Some might be surprised by the secret games in the space domain or the lack of eagerness of governments to make official the existence of non-terrestrial peoples. It must be said that the situation is complex and there are major difficulties.

The reluctance may stem from a desire not to give the public the feeling of a loss of control, both in the governance of countries and in the field of military security.

It can also sign a fear of clashes with far more advanced and powerful military powers or to find oneself in the heart of extraterrestrial dissension and wars with consequences that could be catastrophic.

The danger is also great, for governments to be used as levers of pressure against other Earth nations.

Danger is also present in extraterrestrial conflicts. For example, extraterrestrials in connection with Earth contactees or online groups who worship them, use them as a means of influence against the United Federation of Planets from which they were expelled precisely because of their non-compliance with the Prime Directive. The Andromeda High Councils consider what they share and the way they do it, too radically *alien* at a time in the evolution of humanity when it may not yet be fully capable of accepting the extraterrestrial presence.

It may also be that certain Earth parties, fanatics of power, are reluctant to admit publicly that control of nations and the planet is exercised at another level that does not belong to them.

And in a more humanistic way, the reluctance of governments to engage officially and publicly in frontal contact with different stellar (extraterrestrial) nations expresses the fear of the reaction of a vast majority of the public. They think it would be similar to that of the 1950s when Pt. Eisenhower allowed observers to attend a meeting with stellars (extraterrestrials) all participants deemed, a devastating shock.

ART. 19 – List (not exhaustive) of Agreements and Treaties 1937 - 1991
What treaties have been signed with terrestrial governments?

* For a chronological list supplemented by earthly testimonies, please refer to pages 109 to 118 of the book *ARTIFICIAL* by T.I.M. - Zaor and Viera [84]

N°	Year	Country	Extra-terrestrials	Description
			NON-EXHAUSTIVE LIST OF AGREEMENTS AND TREATIES	
1	Unsuccessful			
	1930	USA	Pleiadians	Contact attempts
	1930	FRANCE	Zeta Reticuli ?	
	1937	RUSSIA	Zeta Reticuli	Contacts and abductions
2	Expired			
	1935	GERMANY	Orion	Nazi-Reptilian Agreement
	1936		Orion Empire	A. Hitler
			Reptilian Dracos	1936 UFO crash with a survivor on board met in person by A. Hitler
3	Expired			
	1947	USA	Zeta Reticuli (*Small Greys*)	Accord / Project Preserve Destiny PPD Pt. H. Truman
	1948		(sent as scouts on behalf of the Reptilian Dracos)	- Roswell + Kenneth Arnold - Contact and installation at military bases - Implementation of the PPD Project Preserve Destiny which will only become effective between 1960 and 1968
4	Unsuccessful			
	1952	USA	Federation of United planets	USAF Base Locations Pt. F. Roosevelt
				Pre-contacts by hacking into the Pentagon

5	Unsuccessful			
	1953	USA	Wolf424 Ummo Ummites (Oomans) & other ETs	Direct Contacts Pt. D. Eisenhower
				Several contacts at 3 separate USAF Air Force bases, with 3 different military groups.
6	Two meetings: proposals rejected			
	1954 18 Feb. & 20-21 Feb.	USA	Federation represented by Pleiadian Antarian Taygetan Five-Star General Rashell of Temmer	Federation Talks – Edwards Air Force Pt. D. Eisenhower
				Two successive meetings. The offer of assistance was refused because no technology was offered. Nuclear disarmament was not considered to be in the best interests of the United States.

* [see history of this meeting in S. 20] |
| 7 | Several meetings: treaty expired December 21st, 2012 | | | |
| | 1954 | USA | Orion Collective

- Zeta-Reticuli Emerthers (Small Greys)

Followed by:

- Reptilian Maytrei (Tall Grays) +
- Albino Malakaks (Tall Whites) +
- Mantis (Insectoids) | Gre(n)ada - Treaty of Granada (Ancient Treaty of the Emerald Alliance) Pt. D. Eisenhower |
| | | | | Exploitation of a limited number of Earthlings – populations tested for genetic compatibility and nominative lists established. People and animal abductions will exceed the initial number by millions (for genetic purposes, or laboratory tests) against the acquisition of advanced technologies and extraterrestrial cooperation. Then in a second time, installation of several alien races, and extension of military bases to accommodate them. (USA bases: Nevada, Colorado, New Mexico, Utah, Mojave Desert, Las Vegas, Nellis Air Force Base, Area51 and Moon bases)

* [see history of this meeting in S. 21] |
| 8 | Extraterrestrial expansion | | | |
| | 1954 Fall | FRANCE | Multi Races | Wave of UFOs so large that it represents 2% of the world directory |

9	Revoked on January 1' 2000			
	1954	RUSSIA	Albino Malakaks	Soviet- Tall White Treaty Pt. K. Voroshilov
			(*Tall Whites*)	Treaty signed by its predecessors in the USSR and revoked by Pt. V. Putin upon taking office.
10	Unsuccessful			
	1954 to 1962	United Nations + Vatican	Wolf424 Ummo Ummites (Oomans) 1953-1962 M45,Pleiadians 1957-1960	Representatives of the main UN countries + Vatican
				Official presentation by the Ummites and other extraterrestrial peoples who share the same ethical values, their positions and warnings to the representatives of the main UN countries as well as to the Vatican which is a permanent observer.
11	Nuclear disarmament			
	1946 1955 1958	United Nations + United Kingdom		Disarmament
				1946 UN calls for elimination of nuclear weapons 1955 Russell-Einstein Manifesto Urging Governments to Resolve Conflicts Peacefully 1958 1st meeting of the United Kingdom Campaign for Nuclear Disarmament – The iconic emblem is one of the most recognized in the world.
12	Expired??			
	1958 1967 1976 1985 1994 2005	USA	Zeta Reticuli (*Small Greys*)	Tau-IX Treaty Pt. G. H.W. Bush
				Established in 1958 (after numerous negotiations since 1954) the treaty was renewed every 9 years in 1967, 1976, 1985, 1994, and the initial negotiations for the latter began in 2003, but were not completed until 2005.
13	Revoked on January 1' 2000			
	1966	RUSSIA	Orion Orion Collective Reptilian Dracos	Soviet-Reptilian Treaty Pt. N. Podgorny
				Treaty signed by its predecessors in the USSR and revoked by Pt. V. Putin upon taking office.

14	Expired: end of August 2021			
	1971	USA	Federation Collective	Desert Accords – 1954 Gre(n)ada or 1958 Tau-IX?
				Non-revelation clause, Prohibition of providing technologies and photos/videos to terrestrial populations.
15	Expired: 1993			
	1989	USA	Zeta Reticuli (*Small Greys*)	Tau-IX Treaty 41st Pt. G. H. Bush I (Sr.)
16	Expired: 1 February 1990			
	1989 Feb. 24 April 18	RUSSIA USA	Wolf424 Ummo Ummites (Oomans)	Mr. Gorbachev, G. Bush Proposals in 32 points in 2 phases. Obligations fulfilled to liberate oppressed peoples. Agreement underlined by the anagram of the General Council of UMMO under the spacecraft seen in Voronezh on 27 September 1989 [Letter D1492] [1]
17	Expired: 1 February 1990			
	1989 27 Sept. 27	United Nations	Wolf424 Ummo Ummites (Oomans)	Meeting with the President of the United Nations (Javier Perez de Cuellar) Non-proliferation of nuclear weapons [Letter D1751] [1]
18	Expired: 1 February 1990			
	1990 April 14	United Nations	Wolf424 Ummo Ummites (Oomans)	Mr. Gorbachev, G. Bush Essen, Germany - 5th meeting [letter D1492] [1]
19	Expired			
	1991 Jan. 9	United Nations	Wolf424 Ummo Ummites (Oomans)	Meeting in Geneva about Iraq [Letter D1751] [1]

Several Heads of State met with extraterrestrial delegations or welcomed them to their military bases, in working groups within their government or research teams. The most famous are the entries N° 6 and N° 7 in the previous table: the encounters between the Pt. D. Eisenhower and several extraterrestrial races that are often confused and presented as one encounter. That is not the case. These are actually 4 landings and 4 meetings (at least): twice two meetings with two delegations of extraterrestrial enemies, the same year, the same month, on the same military bases.

ART. 20 – 1954 – US President D. Eisenhower meets the Nordics
Have extraterrestrials made contact with Heads of State? (Part 1)

There have been numerous attempts at contact and encounters since the 1900s (and long before) but the most well known are those which took place in the USA in February 1954: twice two meetings which took place, on the one hand, with a delegation of Nordics (Blonds) representing the United Federation of Planets and, on the other hand, towards the end of February 1954, with a delegation from Zeta Reticuli (*Small* Greys), sent as scouts, followed subsequently by an Orion Collective: Reptilian-Maytrei (Maitres, *Grand Gris*) and in the months and years to come, the Albino-Mala-kaks (*Tall Whites*) and the Mantis (*Insectoids*).

20.1 – Entry No. 6 on the Treaty List – February 18 and 20-21, 1954 – President D. Eisenhower and the Nordics

• On the Earth side, Dwight D. Eisenhower, Republican Party, who was the 34th president of the United States of America from 1952 to 1969, Five Star General (General of the Army), NATO Supreme Commander since 1950,

• On the extraterrestrial side, Rashell of Temmer, a Pleiadian

111

Nordic woman from Taygeta, one of the nine solar systems in the M45 Taurus Constellation and the Pleiades cluster. Temmer is one of the planets orbiting Taygeta; Five-star General, Supreme Commander and representative of the United Federation of Planets.

Their ranks, statuses and powers are equivalent. But, on the one hand, it is an earthly man and on the other an extraterrestrial woman.

20.2 – Dates and locations of the two meetings

A first meeting took place on Thursday, February 18, 1954, and the second at night, from Saturday to Sunday, from February 20 to 21, 1954, at the Edwards Air Force Base (USAF - formerly Muroc Airfield) located in the Mojave Desert in California, USA. This base was used for spacecraft landings during the first American space missions.

20.3 – Context of the two meetings

The Five Star General Rashell of Temmer was my first Nordic contact which started in June 2016 (and followed others that I had with another race since March). My relationship with her spanned a year, from June 2016 to June 2017. During my first contact with this race, she was accompanied by two young girls she supervised as their Mentor. The two young extraterrestrial girls were learning to develop their skills in communicating with an Earthling (me).

Rashell is of humanoid type, one of the two highest-ranking women of the Taygetan fleet, the other being Five Star General Asket of Temmer; both are also Captain of an attack vessel. They are powerful and determined.

Five Star General Rashell is also a member and ambassador of the United Federation of Planets and the spokesperson for all the member races. So in the extraterrestrial context, he's a powerful, very important and respected person...just like Pt. Eisenhower she's about to meet.

She was 186 years old in 2016 (life expectancy ± 900 years), but like many extraterrestrials, she looks a much younger 35 years-old; very pretty, quite tall, with a pale complexion; Her uniform made of a nanotechnology fits her like a second skin and makes her look to an earthling...somewhat sexy!

President Eisenhower, born in 1890, is 64 years old at the time of the meetings.

From his point of view: he will meet the representative of a delegation from an Extraterrestrial Federation, a woman pretending to come from another planet! And in the context of the Cold War that set in from 1945 until the fall of communist regimes in Europe in 1989, it is a threat to the United States security, which, as the federation had pointed out, is to be taken very seriously.

And these differences between men and women, young-aged, not taking military ranks into account, preconceived notions and suspicion in a context of strong geopolitical tensions, and where, moreover, women have no place in politics, as you will discover, will be a major difficulty in the conduct and outcome of these meetings.

(Hence the importance of this book and to prepare for future official meetings with our space neighbors, which should not be taken lightly).

20.4 – Contact PRIOR to the meetings

A first contact with the American government had already been established in 1947 by the UfoP by breaking into the security of the Pentagon and hacking their radio. The UFoP wanted the American government to understand that it was facing a more powerful entity who had technologies that could breach one of the most secure buildings in the world.

The US was the target country because the Americans were at the forefront of nuclear development and the UFoP was already aware of the presence of German scientists in the Paperclip Project.

* [Operation Paperclip]
Originally referred to as Operation Overcast the operation was conducted by the United States Army Staff at the end of the Second World War to extract and recruit nearly 1,500 German scientists from the military Nazi Germany Complex to fight the USSR and recover the secret weapons of the Third Reich. These scientists carried out research, notably on chemical weapons (Zyklon B), the use of psychotropic drugs such as LSD, space conquest, ballistic missiles

and long-range weapons (flying bombs V1 and V2). [61]

Five-star General Rashell of Temmer was appointed by the UfoP to be the first contact to meet Pt. Eisenhower. It's hard these days to find extraterrestrials who speak English, preferably a man, but at the time it was almost impossible. five-star General Rashell had learned English, which she mastered perfectly; Moreover, her military experience in the context of Earth and her calm attitude were invaluable to start talks or, on the contrary, to react in the event of an attack... The difficulty was that she was female. Would she be taken seriously enough by a powerful Earth man?

The Edwards base (formerly Muroc) in the Mojave Desert, not far from Los Angeles, was chosen because it offers very wide airstrips. The five-star General Rashell and her team knew the base because they had made scouts during a first visit in 1952. The Pt. Eisenhower agreed to meet with them and the date was set for February 28, 1954. It was a Thursday.

20.5 – First meeting with the Nordics on Thursday, February 18, 1954, at Edwards Air Force Base, USA

Five-star General Rashell's diplomatic vessel was at the far end of the trail. For the time being, it was invisible in stealth mode, at approximately 100m altitude and all crew members were monitoring the progress of the operations. Pt. Eisenhower arrived in a Lockheed Electra twin-engine aircraft; He was not alone on the plane and was accompanied by several people, including a member of the CIA. On the ground, there was only one jeep in sight with armed soldiers.

Five-star General Rashell therefore asked Pt. Eisenhower by radio, to kindly remove the soldiers and to disconnect the radars. What was done.

The Federation ship landed slowly for the Pt. Eisenhower and the soldiers to see it with their own eyes and realize it was not the type of craft they knew and to give credibility to their extraterrestrial status. It was a traditional vessel, a discoidal 22 m flying saucer on tree stands. The ramp was lowered.
On his side, the stairs of the presidential plane did the same.

Pt. Eisenhower came down first, dressed in his traditional sand uniform, wearing his military hat and emblems. It wasn't visible, but the extraterrestrial sensors detected that under his uniform, he was armed.

A UfoP crew member came down and stopped on the ship's ramp to observe the scene from a distance, ready to intervene if necessary. The General, in turn, descended from the spaceship, dressed in her traditional one-piece blueish-gray uniform; She didn't have a gun.

They went towards each other and stopped at a distance of 7Ft.

General Rashell said her name and introduced herself as a Representative of the High Council of the United Federation of Planets. He stared at her, doubting her, as a man does when he observes an intriguing woman, who may have been a Russian spy and... fully in his role as Head of State, he said forcefully:

— « *Cut that crap! What do you want?* »

General Rashell offered to help the USA to develop spiritually, to implement a new type of society, free energy, plans of reactors without combustion, and new types of electric transmission.

What the federation wanted in exchange was the dismantling

and destruction of all weapon systems and the total nuclear disarmament of the United States.

He continued to observe her as she argued that if she gave her technologies, the Earthlings would be unable to manage them and that they would be used for destructive purposes. She specified that the ionization of nuclear energy would only bring problems to humanity and that there were better energy options.

The federation was willing to give him these scientific developments in exchange for disarmament.

She added, without hesitation, that the Earthlings were on the road to self-destruction and that wars, pollution, the destruction of wealth and natural resources had to be stopped and they should learn to live together peacefully.

She did not have time to finish her sentence, as Pt. Eisenhower replied emphatically that he could not commit himself to it because the Russians would have the upper hand against the United States.

General Rashell insisted that the Russians, too, should proceed with the disarmament and destroy all their weapons.

Pt. Eisenhower welcomed her comments with extreme distrust, especially the major condition of nuclear disarmament. He believed that by accepting these conditions, they would leave the USA powerless in the face of a Russian or extraterrestrial threat that since 1953, you will see shortly thereafter, became more and more obvious.

He went on, saying, dissatisfied, that his meeting with her was part of a communist plot to disarm the United States and without delay, with a loud voice, he put an end to the conversation. He made a namaste by leaning slightly, turned the heels and resumed the plane.

General Rashell boarded the Federation ship and everyone parted.
End of the first meeting.

20.6 Second meeting with the Nordics, in the night from Saturday 20th to Sunday 21st, February 1954, at Edwards Air Force base, USA

As soon as General Rashell returned to her ship, her crew and the members of the federation who accompanied her made a debriefing. They decided to contact Pt. Eisenhower immediately and told him that he had to think twice about their offer, pretending—even if it was inaccurate, and they were using it as leverage—that their next appointment was with the Kremlin.

New threat to which Pt. Eisenhower replied by agreeing to meet them a second time, two days later, on the night from Saturday February 20th to Sunday 21st, 1954.

This second meeting took place like the previous one, on the same Edwards base. This time, there were many more people and military personnel, both in buildings, in radars and in jeeps. No one was armed, or at least there was no gun pointed at them. The Pt. Eisenhower came out much faster and General Rashell repeated what she had already said, by specifying that unfortunately the federation could not offer anything else out of respect for the Prime Directive and the Laws governing terrestrial and non-terrestrial space relations.

Pt. Eisenhower got carried away saying she wasn't an extra-terrestrial, and accused her of being a Nazi, and a member of the Vril Society, that she and her companions were hiding in Antarctica and that they had been spotted by the CIA intelligence services who had recognized her in photos dating from the 1930s and 1940s.

Then, without giving her time to answer, he turned around, boarded his plane and disappeared.
The meeting ended again with a fiasco.

For an uninformed outside observer, the situation seemed very ambiguous. A president who, in order to face a threat to the security of the United States and who did not know in advance that he was going to meet a pretty young woman, even though she was a 186-year-old Five Star General, had organized a family vacation in the area and had told the press following him that he had gone to his dentist. If this meeting were disclosed, the newspapers would have made the front page of a president who was lying, cheating on his wife, and moreover, had taken his family to cover his wrongdoings! Bigre!

General Rashell did not meet him again in several other attempts at talks that took place, organized by the Pleiadians between 1957 and 1960 and the Ummites between 1953 and 1962 – all of which proved to be as brief and fruitless.

[Note: Pt. Eisenhower was probably referring to Maria Orsic (Oršić, Ortisch, Orschitsch, Marija Orsitsch), Austrian medium, priestess of the Vril Society, who prophesied the crash of a UFO in Freiburg in 1936. There was a survivor on board, whom the Führer had said after meeting him in person: « I saw the superman...and I was shaking in front of him! » Thanks to this event, German military and scientific technology will experience an extraordinary development. Maria Orsic was behind the development of the first Nazi UFO – Note from the Author : this superman may have been a Reptilian-Draco shape-shifter in human form].

ART. 21 – 1954 – US President D. Eisenhower meets
with Zeta Reticuli
Have extraterrestrials made contact with Heads of State? (Part 2)

When he met General Rashell, the palpable tension the Pt. Eisenhower was feeling was probably due to the geopolitical situation on Earth as much as to the announcement of extraterrestrial ships orbiting Earth. In 1953, a few months earlier, American astronomers had discovered large objects in space that were heading for Earth. They thought they were asteroids.

But their extensive research showed that they actually were spacecrafts. When they reached Earth, they placed themselves in a very high geosynchronous orbit around the equator and did not move. Their intentions were not known. And that wasn't very reassuring.

21.1 – Entry No. 7 – Late February 1954
Pt. Eisenhower meets the Zeta Reticuli

The SIGMA and PLATO projects were set up, to communicate with this race of extraterrestrials using radio communications and a binary computer language; that's how they managed to organize a first landing and a first face-to-face meeting in the Mojave desert and a member of the extraterrestrial delegation remained on Earth as a token of their willingness to sign a treaty with the USA.

This volunteer was none other than a royal member of the Reptilian-Draco Empire, His Royal Highness, Omnipotent Eminence Krlll.

The PLATO project was then in charge of the diplomatic relations and for implementing the terms of the treaty. The Americans were interested in advance attack technologies, propulsion techniques and spacecrafts.

At the end of February 1954, after the unsuccessful meeting with five Star General Rashell of Temmer and the Nordic Delegation, the Zetas Emerthers made a second landing (which was therefore the 4th during this period) on the same Edwards Base where the terms of engagement between the two nations were ratified and the treaty signed. They explained to Pt. Eisenhower that their race was dying and they would not survive. So they traded some of their technology for the right to harvest human and animal DNA and do genetic testing.

They promised not to sign a treaty with another nation. But they did not respect this part of the Treaty by getting closer to Russia and they exceeded their rights to remove a limited number of humans, for the purposes of medical examinations and human development monitoring! They specified, but failed too, not to injure earthlings and to return them exactly to the place they had been abducted from, under the exact conditions they had been taken. They pledged that no abductees would remember they had been kidnapped.

The US agreed to provide the list of people to be abducted. As you have already discovered in the testimony of Sergeant Dan Sherman, between 1960 and 1968, these treaty clauses were activated, within Project Preserve Destiny, and random tests began to be carried out, to determine the genetic compatibility of populations and nominative lists were established. They were short at first; But the stellars (extraterrestrials) extended their hold to other nations, beyond the terms of the treaties that bound them to the USA, and the lists of abductions spread in many countries, by the millions.

It also turned out that the technologies the USA had received were faulty. When the American government demanded further scientific information, these extraterrestrial races agreed to give them in exchange for the construction of underground bases where the exchange of technologies would be done jointly.

Their method of colonizing an already inhabited world is to build a first underground operational base, then gradually extend it to the entire planet by constructing networks of tunnels connecting key tactical bases. The beginning of this colonizing hold is achieved thanks to a handful of leaders, institutions and organizations on the surface, to which absolute power is granted by the extraterrestrials.

The bases were therefore extended or built in Utah, Colorado, New. Mexico, Arizona, and in the Mojave Desert: area 51.

The land where area 51 was built was bought in 1955, a few months after the meeting with the Zeta Delegation. This base is a land base, but there also is an underwater part to it; This is why it is managed by the American Navy: it holds nuclear submarines and is directly connected to underwater networks, from the Santa Monica Bay, near Los Angeles. From there, submarines can reach Antarctica and other bases scattered around the world.

In the secrecy of services deployed as the layers of an onion, in the heart of the American military complexes and consequently of the United States, which the extraterrestrials were now joining in a spaceship, using the Moon as an intermediate stopover and experimental base [see ART. 11/Sherman & 33/Cloning Centers]...the fate of millions of abducted Earthlings and animals had just been sealed!

ART. 22 – Presentation: exoprotocols, precedence, statutes, titles
How to address stellars (extraterrestrials)?

Taking into account the Treaty N° 7, the presentation of some lineages of extraterrestrials, their morphologies, their languages, their temperaments, their statuses in the hierarchies of royal, civil, military, or spiritual seniority you may conclude very rightly, that according to the circumstances, there is a way to introduce oneself, to behave or to communicate that is specific to each extraterrestrial race.

On earth, the way of introducing oneself, of dressing, what is said, the relations between men and women, the position of the interlocutors in a group, the precedence and protocols, structure the civil meetings and even more, the royal, governmental, religious or military relations. It is the same with stellars (extraterrestrials).

When the official meetings that took place with Five Star General Rashell of Temmer and the delegation of Nordics, if the American President D. Eisenhower had not adopted a colloquial and informal way of addressing her; if he and the CIA personnel advising him had been aware that military protocols had to be taken into account, the General's titles and status – especially in the case of General Rashell, who is one of the highest-ranking representatives in a matriarchal society where women have power and are militarily far more powerful than men on Earth – and if they had considered her at the same level as the President himself, the meetings would probably have taken a very different pace and the treaties would have been of a completely different nature.

> [Author's Note: This comment is not a criticism, but a simple observation in view of my experience in this field and an invitation to take into account the points mentioned in our future relations and official negotiations especially at the diplomatic level of government.]

22.1 – Earth Precedence

Protocol precedence is created by use, established by rules and governed by laws. They are enshrined in the constitutions of each country.

The order of precedence is a symbolic hierarchy defining, the order of official personalities during public ceremonies.

They are not the same for a civilian, the Chief of an indigenous tribe, the Emperor of Japan, the King of Saudi Arabia, the Queen of England, the President of a nation or a High Military or Religious Leader.

In France, precedence and honors are governed by the 13 September 1989 Decree No. 89-655 on public ceremonies, precedence, civil and military honors. [67]

Within a rank, the oldest stands ahead his peers or, on equal seniority, the oldest. A King or President is always at the center of a ceremony. And the right side takes precedence over the left side. For example, during official meetings with *Her Royal Highness,* Her Majesty Queen Elizabeth II, reverence (for women) or bow down (for men) is mandatory and the address is *Your Majesty*; during a dinner, Her Majesty first addresses the person seated on her right, then, the person seated on her left; when Her Majesty rises, everyone rises; When Her Majesty has finished her meal, so does everyone.

In civilian life: a man climbs a staircase before a woman and goes down after her; On the sidewalk he must stand on the side of the roadway; He opens a door and let her pass; or one does not address an elderly person or a teenager in the same way or using the same type of wording; You don't interrupt a person talking, as everybody does nowadays, it's rude and disrespectful.

22.2 – Extraterrestrial precedence

As on Earth, the extraterrestrial precedence is extremely varied according to the lineages. But as on Earth there are bases that must not be circumvented:

- deference,

- respect,

- titles and statutes,

- a somewhat formal language register,

- autonomy,

- calm, and a neutral, non-emotional attitude, no excitement

- do not touch the interlocutors (no kissing, no shaking hands),

- speak when invited.

22.3 – Tips for Introducing Yourself

This is the advice I received from Five Star General Asket of Temmer, when I sought the opportunity to intervene as an Earth Mediator, during the sessions of the Andromeda High Council within the United Federation of Planets, by receiving the issues discussed that concerned the Earth. I also wanted to establish contact with other races, especially with the Andromedans.

I had to do it in writing, and I was wondering what the criteria would be that would tilt the scales in my direction so that they would accept my participation and see me as a credible and serious interlocutor. It was like sending an application to be selected for a high-level position.

The criteria are different.

Here is the response that the General sent me in writing, on December 15, 2016, after the first nine months of contacts:

• Your references •

« The Andromeda High Council was composed at the time of 12 different species or subspecies that have different evaluation criteria. But the part of your experiences that have the most weight, those to which all races will adhere are: »

• Spirituality •

« What they consider to be very important is your spiritual development, your level of consciousness and everything that has to do with Enlightenment, your training or your experiences in this field, both personal as a

134

forest monk and as a guide to help others, and the books or articles you have written on these topics. »

• Moral and Ethical Values •

« What is really important to all members of the UFoP is who you are as a person, your moral and ethical values, how you think, your journey through the process of enlightenment: It's really the heart of what they're looking for when they meet a new person. »

• University Degrees vs. Being a Mother •

« Your many degrees up to your Ph.D, obtained in Earth universities are not considered important; it is preferable to mention only the one of the highest level.

For them, the fact that you're a mother is far more important than having a degree. Not all extraterrestrial parents educate their children themselves. So that you have done this is considered *service to others*; you have cared for another person for 28 years to date.

That said, anything you can say about yourself will be invaluable to them and to their decision-making, but I have noticed that they consider overeducated Earthlings with many high-level degrees, as particularly *matrixed* (being an integral part of the terrestrial system and generally not open to extraterrestrials and new scientific concepts). But of course, it varies from person to person; they do not generalize and apprehend people for what they are. »

• Language and Education •

« The part about your experience in Language, Communication and Education Sciences, in large academic groups of several hundred people or in conferences, is also valuable for them, because you have experience in teaching traditional concepts as well as new ones; you know how students react, their attention span when you teach, their motivations, etc. »

• Arts •

« Your Graphic and Visual Arts training and their applications within artistic communities demonstrate your creativity in which they will be interested. »

• Multicultural •

« Your travels to many countries can also be very useful especially because you are used to and accept multiculturality and you are therefore open to the plurality of extraterrestrial races that can sometimes be very different. »

22.4 – Written Submission

Based on these valuable insights, I created a file in English (since my contacts did not speak French) specifically for members of the UfoP ; It included:

- a six-page cover letter,

- my Curriculum Vitae, was revised and included the aspects highlighted by Five-Star General Asket and it did not start with the list of my diplomas as is usually done when applying for a job on Earth, 1.5 pages,

- A copy of two books I published online on meditation and enlightenment (several hundred pages).

My Mentor Zen translated the entire file into Andromedan, including the two books and the General Asket accompanied by Zen, presented it at a UfoP plenary session.

My candidacy as a Mediator was accepted.

The Andromedans asked me for a second letter which motivated my request to be in direct contact with one of them. Zen translated it. And in another session, the Andromedan Moranae of Andromeda (Alex Collier's contact) offered to be my contact.

All of this was endorsed by the Andromeda High Council and by the 12-nation members of the federation. And so began my *mission* as *The InterStellar Mediator.*

I would suggest you start thinking about who you are, put yourself in the same position I was and create your own file. If it is never used in writing, it will allow you to become aware of the elements that are important in your life and that will also be important for stellars (extraterrestrials) in future interplanetary relations. And you will be ready to introduce yourself orally in a one-to-one or a diplomatic context.

22.5 – Oral Presentation

With the points of precedence in mind, this is the most respected and secure way you can introduce yourself. Do not deviate from it because you will not really know who your interlocutors are at first. It will deepen as contacts last. Always stay on a constant benevolent alert, because some very attractive races, are seductive as well as manipulative. Watch your reactions and don't get carried away:

- deference, respect, a somewhat formal language register,

- observance of the statutes (royal, military, spiritual or civil); use the titles,

- a calm attitude, self-mastery, above all no excitement,

- do not touch your interlocutors, do not move your arms forward, as this can be seen as a sign of aggression by some races, no namaste, no hugging, or shaking hands: step forward to the designated place, bow as Japanese do with your head bent, arms down near your body,

- do not laugh or smile unless one of the participants is humorous,

- Stand up and look up at the person speaking to you,

- Don't speak until you're invited.

Here is the formal way Andromedans present themselves when they enter a meeting room:

« I am [First name, surname] of [country] [solar system] Sol 13, [planet] Terra 3, [§22.3: main criteria] ...[n°1] [n°2] [n°3]... - This is the way and custom when one enters my space that permission is required. »

The reason you have to say the second part of this sentence is that not only is it the Andromedan tradition but your interlocutors are ALL telepathic. Especially the Ancient Andromedans Sages who are very developed in this area. They grab the content of your brain to read it (it will give you the impression that it has just been abruptly emptied.)

All races honor this request and will not read your thoughts if you tell them that they must seek your permission before entering your mental space. This shows that you know the rules, that you are able to repel such attempts and you have great spiritual mastery.

22.6 – Six Inappropriate Behaviors

1. **Do not complain**, never ask for help unless you are invited to do so, because this would mean you are not autonomous; it is only when it is certain that the human race will be stable, survive and reach maturity WITHOUT external help that the stellars (extraterrestrials) will put an end to Earth isolation and welcome Earthlings within their communication systems. And conversely, do not adopt an attitude of veneration, because the level of exchange would not be balanced and certain extraterrestrial races would take advantage of it.

2. **Do not express anger**, when you expose your ideas or convictions because the older races consider that you are fully realized when you are no longer carried away by your emotions. The older and wiser the races, the less they express emotions in favor of logic and reason.

3. **Do not engage a person**, and don't call them *Brother* or *Sister* unless they do it first with you ; instead use their titles.

4. **Do not place your hand on the other person's chest** as the Ummites do. The chest or breast is considered extremely intimate and touching it would be considered inappropriate. The same goes for the Ummites who usually lay their hand on the person's chest. It would be a violation of an Earthling intimacy (especially for a woman). I suggest everyone uses the Japanese-style bow.

5. **Do not assault anyone**, either physically or verbally, unless you have to fight an attack. In any case, your thoughts and intentions will be known even before you express them.

6. **Don't panic** if there is frontal contact, stay calm. You will be monitored 24/7 whatever you do and whatever you think. You'll have to get used to it. Everything will be recorded and explanations will be requested if necessary.

ART. 23 – Warning: Abnormal Trauma
Is there any danger in coming into contact with extraterrestrials?

People who have been abducted warn the public against any attempt to contact extraterrestrials. They claim that contactees may end up physically injured or even die, as some races are malicious or manipulative and may victimize humans in different ways; there are also accidents.

The relationship of a contactee with his extraterrestrial interlocutors depends on the degree of clarity, knowledge and mental attitude. Some uninformed people will interpret it negatively and others positively. In either case, it may be the starting point for a profound reflection on life and the nature of reality.

Many people who have been contacted or abducted develop physical distress syndromes such as chronic fatigue, immune disorders and gynecological abnormalities. Psychological disorders may also result, such as depression, or signs of post-traumatic stress disorder (PTSD); They are categorized as *Abnormal Trauma* and must be taken very seriously if you develop them during or after extraterrestrial contact. It is recommended to contact a therapist or hypnotherapist specialized in these areas:

1. Abuse in the Quest for Contact with Extraterrestrials

•UFO channeling groups and cults, in person or online,

•sectarian groups worshipping or hating extraterrestrials,

2. Injuries from Contact or Abduction

•individual UFO sightings with abduction, erased memory, missing time,

•abduction and/or extraterrestrial visits, with multi-generational family involvement,

•visits of space *brothers* or *sisters*, benevolent or malicious,

•dreamlike, telepathic or channeling contacts,

3. Military Abductions

•persons abducted by the army or other agencies, for questioning following extraterrestrial contacts,

•trained military personnel for secret missions that they are never allowed to talk about.

ART. 24 – Impact of Official Extraterrestrial Contact
What would be the impacts of contact with extraterrestrials?

The official disclosure of an extraterrestrial contact would see the development of a set of changes which would vary according to the attitude of the interlocutors and their level of aggression or benevolence, their level of spirituality, their attitude towards earthly humanity, their technology, the level of communication. Studies have been carried out to try to define the implications of such contact.

In 1961, seven years after the signing of the Treaty of Gre(n)ada, the Brookings Report, a study of public reactions to the announcement of the existence of extraterrestrials, measured the implications of such an announcement at government level for space industries, in international affairs and foreign policies, in communication systems, in science and religions and the public reactions. The conclusions of prudence that were issued, have since determined the policy of the governments with regard to extraterrestrial intelligence and defense secrecy.

In 2017, the United States Department of Defense confirmed the existence of the *Unidentified Phenomena Task Force*, UAPTF and a program to standardize the compilation and restitution of observations of unidentified aerial phenomena. This program, like the previous ones, is under the responsibility of the Secretary of Defense for Intelligence who works in collaboration with the Naval Intelligence Bureau.

Following a hearing in the Senate in June 2020, Marco Rubio, Republican Senator in Florida, asked that the UFO observations collected by the US Navy, including those archived by the Pentagon, be made public.

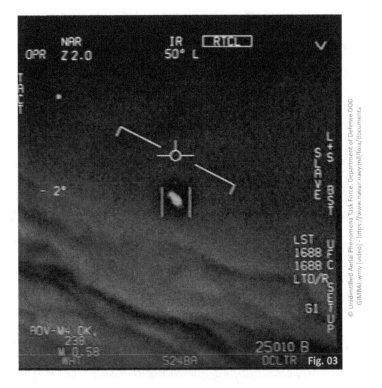

Fig. 03

The Task Force on Unidentified Phenomena focused on 144 observations made between 2004 and 2021 by the US armed forces, primarily by naval personnel and their findings were published in a report on June 25, 2021, with three unclassified Navy videos, one taken in November 2004 and the other two in January 2015. The conclusions of the working group state that the aerial phenomena observed in the videos remain characterized as *unidentified*.

In response to the report of the UAPTF working group, the international academic and civil ufological community, expressed its independent assessment of the report and committed to coordinating the consistent integration of their results in scientific papers and related cross-disciplinary areas, to advance understanding and innovation in this area of research in an academic manner. [10]

The research is organized around three research themes:

1. A group of scientists and academics accompanied by civilians adopted an anthropological approach,

2. A military group, study and postulate that secret, unconventional technologies are in the hands of several na-

tions and that they look like UFOs,

3. A group of ufologists analyze the hypothesis of extraterrestrial existence, a genetic and cultural intervention, and
direct contact or experience with stellars (extraterrestrials).

Chapter 3

EXTRATERRESTRIAL CATEGORIZATION OF EARTHLINGS

This chapter presents how stellars (extraterrestrials) forms of life on a planet are classified. Earthlings, Homo sapiens, develop their species identity through two main currents:

- **creationism,** humans created by God, is a current conveyed by family traditions, religions and sacred books,

- **evolutionism,** humans descending from monkeys, is a current conveyed by conventional research promoting scientific, material and historical naturalism.

If stellars (extraterrestrials) respect these classifications as indigenous expressions of evolution, they categorize the different planetary life forms, in a completely different way: it is the *soul* as a whole and a person's incarnations that they take into account.

ART. 25 – Categorization of Homo sapiens
How do stellars (extraterrestrials) study Earthlings?

Stellars (extraterrestrials) study the different categories of humans on Earth as mere animal species in their natural biotopes, as they do for any planet they discover or develop. They analyze Homo sapiens, in various fields, to better understand behaviors, lifestyles, thoughts and reactions. Generally speaking, Earthlings are not considered to be a full-fledged race, but a combination of many other hominid races; these notions of *sub-race* echo, to that of the Greek sophists, Byron or Goethe, the culmination of Dostoyevsky's nihilism in *Crime and Punishment* (1866) *[27]*, or Gobineau's Negro phobic or Aryan stereotypes in *Essay on the Inequality of the Human Races* [30] – which were widespread in science and politics from the 19th to the 20th century, and attempted to justify colonialism in the name of evolution and progress.

The *Über-mensch* the *superhuman* popularized by Nietzsche in *Human, All Too Human* (1878) [59], or in *Thus Spoke Zarathustra* (1883) [59] continues to be perpetuated today, under the features of super-heroes, super-soldiers and the futurist biotechnologically augmented or cyborgized humans.

In line with the figures of the Etorthan Statistical Society (*Tall Grays With Flat Nose)* originating from the constellation of Orion, Alpha

Orionis, star α Orionis Betelgeuse, planet Ethort, they assert that the total Earth population is 4.4 billion, not 7.8 billion people. This figure does not include stellar (extraterrestrial) hominids from other planets living on Earth, who are:

- on temporary missions, in social, psychological, spiritual, political or military operations,

- on a permanent mission, in expeditionary groups living alone or in colonies scattered on the surface or in underground bases throughout the world,

- or defectors or political refugees who have settled on Earth after fleeing the regime of their planet or repressive, totalitarian and dictatorial extraterrestrial societies.

Most extraterrestrials are aligned with the Etorthan statistics of 10% or 778,000,000 (778 million) Earthlings who have a *soul* of which a significant percentage is represented by natives (EarthSeeds), stellar emissaries (StarSeeds), stellar Crawls-ins, stellar Walk-ins, stellar Walk-downs (expeditionaries) hybrids and hubrids, as well as earthlings of multiple other origins and endemic communities.

The remaining 90% would be made up of *soulless* people, bionic people, clones or synthetic humanoid borgs programmed and controlled by artificial intelligence in a global matrix.

ART. 26 – The Natives (EarthSeeds)
What are the different types of humans on Earth?

The Natives (Earthseeds) are Homo sapiens type Earthlings.

One of the most debated issues in paleoanthropology is the origins of the Homo sapiens species, anatomically modern humans (AMHs), and the fate of the Neanderthals who preceded them. According to the stellars (extraterrestrial), human origins on Earth are varied and have evolved simultaneously in different biotopes.

According to stellars (extraterrestrial) Homo sapiens Human is a composite of 22 species of hominids that have reproduced by inter-fecondation and hybridization between protohumans, interstellar species installed on Earth, and archaic and modern humans.

The human species has developed in two ways:

- natural: protohumans or previously unidentified hominid species were first implanted on Earth by Dieslientiplex (Arcturian lineage) and Ethortans (Draconian lineage). These species evolved naturally, through gentle transition, thanks to the interbreeding between protohumans and multiple hominids before the Denisovians and the Neanderthals and *in fine*, between Neanderthal women and modern Sapiens, present in the same territories at the same time;

- artificial: by artificial hybridization essentially (but not only) carried out by the Draconian Reptilian lineages.

The Neanderthals are said to have mixed with the Sapiens by miscegenation (crossbreeding). This hypothesis is supported by evidence of changes in late Neanderthal morphology demonstrating continuity of anatomical or behavioral characteristics. This hypothesis is supported by Condemi *et al.* (2014):

> "We're looking at the mandible of Riparo Mezzena... Mitochondrial DNA analysis performed on this jaw and other cranial fragments found at the same stratigraphic level has led to the identification of the only genetically typed Neanderthal of the Italian peninsula and has confirmed through direct dating that it belongs to a late Neanderthal. ... [The] study of the Mezzena jaw shows that the chin region is similar to that of other late Neanderthals which display a much more modern morphology ... In our view, this change in morphology...supports the hypothesis of anatomical change...and...a certain degree of interbreeding with AMHs [Anatomically Modern Humans]... [and] a non-abrupt phylogenetic transition for this period in Europe. [19]"

Homo sapiens developed in parallel with distant stellar (extraterrestrial) human ancestors, originating from multiple solar systems, originating from the constellation of Lyra (M56-M57-Kepler 62), the constellation of Taurus (M45) or the southern constellation of the Reticle:

"In the constellation of Lyra the solar system Vega has several beautiful planets that [the invaders] coveted... While this invasion was taking its course and populations were exterminated, women and children separated, men killed in battle or by brutal and savage force, or used as slaves, the Lyrians who were already interstellar, They sought refuge on other planets and left in small groups to be more likely to survive in small communities. They flew to other solar systems mainly to M33 the constellation of the Triangle, M45 the constellation of Taurus and SOL13 our solar system where they arrived on Earth as a spacecraft 40,000 years ago.

The Lyrians who look like Earthlings, but larger, more muscular and have a longer life expectancy, are a part of our ancestors; they developed at the same time as the Neanderthals and Denisovians and the ancient peoples who regarded them as Gods; the Lyrians, as well as the Neanderthals, lived mainly underground to protect themselves; they inscribed their origins in the shelters they occupied, as well as their solar system and planet, when and how they arrived. This point explains the level of astronomical knowledge that some peoples we think *primitive* have left everywhere in the world, in the heart of caves covered with wall art or buildings carved directly into the rock massif by extraction with a technology that primitive peoples did not possess. The habitats were separate; some places belonged to the Neanderthals or the Denisovians and others to the Lyrians. [84]"

ART. 27 – The Stellar Crawl-ins
What is a crawl-in?

Inner development and maturation boost *souls* to integrate matter. There are two main ways for stellar or emissary *souls* (starSeeds) to incarnate on Earth: at birth (crawl-in), or by infiltrating an existing human body (walk-in).

A crawl-in is a *soul* born on Earth from human biological parents. Integration occurs 3 weeks after conception. When integrating matter, the soul feels like *jumping* down from hyperspace into a very dense physical body; Only remote parts of the extraterrestrial origins are carried over.

ART. 28 – The Stellar Walk-ins
What is a Walk-in?

A walk-in is *a stellar roommate,* a *soul* that incarnates using a for-med body, sometimes as an adult, and at different ages - example:

. 0 to 33 years old: a crawl-in uses the body from birth to 33 years old, then it will leave to return to its original body...

. 33 years to death, a second *soul,* a walk-in this time, will inte-grate the same body.

A *soul* will want to experience birth and not death, or vice versa, another will want to experience death and not birth. Then a third *soul* will not want to experience birth or death, but will want to live a certain number of years on Earth to accomplish a mission. This body will therefore be shared successively by three *souls.*

Incarnation in a fully developed body allows the most advanced soul to carry out a mission without having to go through the two decades of maturation that Earthlings need to reach adulthood.

But sometimes, several *souls* occupy the same body simultaneously. They are often synchronized and work together to take charge of different aspects of their common mission.

It is said that *souls* enter or switch during a period of intense personal problems, or during an accident or a trauma. The individual retains the memories of the original *soul*, but personality and abilities change considerably and often are geared to helping humanity.

ART. 29 - Stellar Walk-downs
What is a walk-down?

A walk-down is a stellar (extraterrestrial), male or female, that fly down in an actual spaceship for specific temporary missions that can last from a few hours to a few years. A crew in a shuttle or a pilot in a spaceship will drop the extraterrestrial expeditionary in an isolated place on earth, then leave.

Many interstellar species cannot do this, as not all races possess the phenotypic or morphological criteria of humanoid type. If they do, it can be difficult for them to breathe oxygen, drink Earth water or ingest food, often containing toxins that could make them sick.

They must also be able to speak Earth languages and the language used in the country where they landed or at least know written and oral English, and finally, their ways of thinking or expressing themselves are so different that even if they look like Earthlings, They can still surprise their interlocutors and be spotted.

In this case, stellars (extraterrestrials) prefer to go back and forth between a mothership and Earth: they drop off the authorized crew members in the morning and pick them up in the evening from safe houses or places they use for this purpose. They also sometimes use ships stationed in isolated places that are in stealth mode and invisible to Earth populations.

ART. 30 - Hybrids
What are hybrids? Does hybridization exist between humans and animals?

Stellar hybrids have both human and extraterrestrial genetic coding and are extraterrestrial *souls*.

Hybridization is the natural or artificial crossing of two individuals, plants or animals of different species, breeds or varieties.

30. 1 - Hybrid between a Homo sapiens and a stellar (extraterrestrial)

A hybrid of the *Homo* genus is the result of crossing two species of hominids with similar characteristics, originating from two planets with similar biotopes, able to procreate a fertile progeny to ensure the perpetuation of a lineage.

30.2 - Conditions for hybridization between two species of the *Homo genus* living on two different planets

For this type of crossbreeding to be a reality, let's move away from Earth geocentrism which considers that only planet Earth is inhabited, and is, therefore, the primal place of human spatial expansion, by introducing the following ideas:

(a) planets may have more or less advanced stages of development. For example in 2016–2017 the Andromedans were carrying out surveys of a planet they had newly discovered: the planet was devoid of population and wildlife was neither aggressive nor predatory;

On the contrary, other planets they studied were already developed and inhabited, but they had not yet reached the industrial era,

(b) exoplanets with biotopes similar to those on Earth are already inhabited, but they are yet to be discovered,

(c) prior to becoming endemic on Earth, protohumans or archaic humans were implanted by interstellar races that have the skills of caring and developing new planets; in particular the Dieslientiplex (the Arcturians) also called *The Gardeners* and the Ethortans as expert geneticists,

(d) other species of hominids having the same characteristics as Earthlings had already reached interstellarity; they left on space exploration missions or had to leave as a result of colonization. These peoples landed on Earth and developed colonies and settlements. They brought their knowledge, especially astronomical, their techniques, their technologies, their value systems,

(e) these same species have been able to persist by interfering and crossbreeding with endemic proto-species,

f) despite the eminent American biologist Ernst Mayr's statement claiming there is « never more than one Homo species existing at the same time, » there would have been at least two human typologies: endogenous (they developed on Earth) and exogenous (they came from another planet) and these species evolved simultaneously for more or less prolonged periods in close proximity within the same biotopes.

30.3 - Reproduction is a biological process that generates new organisms from pre-existing individuals of a specific species. For the offspring to be fertile, it reproduction must occur only between individuals of the same species. For example, a lion and a lioness.

For a chromosome matching incompatibility issue, there is no crossbreeding between distinct and distant species such as an eagle and a butterfly, or a camel and a whale, or a baobab and a giraffe.

30.4 - Natural hybridization is the reproduction between two distinct species, but close enough from a physiological point of view, that resort to a normal process of sexual reproduction. But the female hybrid will be little or not fertile at all and the male hybrid will be sterile; It is the case of the zonkey, a hybrid between a male zebra and a female donkey or the leopon, a hybrid between a male leopard and a lioness.

zonkey   leopon

Fig. 05 ©Zdor & Viern, 2021

30.5 - Artificial hybridization may ignore certain norms and be caused by using techniques of fusion of two species to form a new hybrid inheriting selected genetic properties of the two species of origin. Intraspecific hybrids will generally be fertile, while interspecific hybrids will be poorly fertile or even sterile.

Similarly, if certain species, for example, Earthlings and Pleiadians or Earthlings and Ummites, are physically compatible because they belong to close hominid species, chromosome pairing is not and mating does not allow the birth of fertile hybrids or the emergence of a new Terro-Pleiadian or Terro-Ummite lineage.

Stellars (extraterrestrials) as well as scientists on Earth, have developed tools to modify the genetic makeup of organisms by removing, introducing or replacing DNA. In genetic engineering, sequencing and genomic editing techniques, such as the CRISPR-Cas9 system developed since the 2000s by French researcher Emanuelle Charpentier, [14] 2020 Nobel Prize in Chemistry with American Jennifer Doudna, allow for the modification of DNA sequences and thus genetic information to incorporate new traits such as the Humanzee hybrid.

30.6 - The *Humanzee* hybrid known by the English portmanteau word *Humanzee* [*human* and *zee* from chimpan*zee,* and from *ci-mpenzi* used in Vili (Bantu language of Congo] is the result of research proposals that have never been undertaken, of human – monkey hybridization.

The idea was advanced in 1910, by the Russian biologist, Director of the Division of Physiology of the Institute of Experimental Veterinary Medicine in Moscow, who was a specialist in interspecies artificial insemination and hybridization, Prof. Il'ia I. Ivanov; his objective was to determine the degree of phylogenetic relationship between monkeys and humans, similar to those that were later made by researcher J. M. Bedford who discovered that human semen could penetrate the outer membranes of a protective ovum of a long-arm tree monkey: the gibbon (Hylobatidae). [8]

Humanzee

© Zaor & Viera, 2021.
Courtesy Liza Phoenix 2006-Wikipedia   Fig. 06

In their article on hybridization and the Research Centre on Sukhum Primates in Russia, Fridman and Bowden [28], describe Ivanov's research in the context of the time and how Ivanov's intentions were wrongly distorted:

« In the late 1990s, Ivanov was bitterly attacked by science fiction writer E. Parnov [63] who claimed to have had access to research archives that had been classified...

The most disturbing distortion...was the sensational *revelation* in the press and on national television that Ivanov had crossed humans with monkeys to breed new primate races... After Parnov published the provocative stories, a series of similar reports appeared in the press and on television, where the theme of species hybridization was associated with the stories of the abominable snowman...

and aliens from outer space. In one of these TV shows, Parnov portrays himself as the Sukhum Primate Center History Expert and specified that - « it is unlikely that anyone could guess what was really going on there during those long years. »

The truth is that since its creation and throughout its 80 years of history [the Sukhum Primate Center] has never made any attempt to hybridize monkeys, let alone crossing monkeys with humans.

Professor Ivanov had proposed crossing experiments very early on, but his objective was simply to determine the degree of phylogenetic relationship between monkeys and humans. There was no absurd idea of creating a « new race of humans »...

In the spring of 1927, before the establishment of the center, he had conducted an experiment in Africa involving the artificial insemination of three female chimpanzees with human semen. The attempt took place under formidable conditions in Conakry, then part of French Guinea, in West Africa. Two of the animals died on the ship between Dakar and Marseille. The autopsies of both, conducted on the ship, and the third, by a pathologist from a local hospital in Sukhum, re-vealed no evidence of conception. The experiment ended before the center existed. [28]"

ART. 31 - The Hubrids
Do kidnappings (abductions) have anything to do with hybridization? Does hybridization exist between two extraterrestrial species?

The word *Hubrid* is a portmanteau word coined by the American historian and ufologist David M. Jacobs from the words *human* and *hybrid*. The Hubrids are the result of an Earthling-Extraterrestrial cross-breeding program, carried out by the latter, in a vast secret and global infiltration program of Earth society, whose purpose is said to be the control of the Earth. They have both human and extraterrestrial genetic coding, but they are *terrestrial souls* (unlike extraterrestrial only hybrids).

Jacobs says that some of the patients or subjects with whom he worked were abducted to teach hubrids how to blend into human society so as not to be differentiated from Earthlings.

Stellars (extraterrestrials) use genetic manipulation for different purposes:

. populating a virgin planet with species of hominids specific to the planet;

. Repopulate a destroyed planet where the human species is extinct;

. Inject new reproductive dynamics for an extinct species;

. Increase, correct the physical, behavioral or mental features of an existing species;

. Transform reproductive mechanisms;

. to colonize a planet by force of arms, relocate the existing populations and empty the planet, then develop a new species adapted to the needs and uses of the conqueror.

There are plenty of testimonies and numerous stories of stellar (extraterrestrial) abductions report large-scale reproductive programs: telepathic communication, paralysis, amnesia, *small greys* with large black eyes, copulations, physical examinations, extraction of eggs, sperm, as well as fetal extraction and implantation.

The most famous cases of sexual intercourse and hybridization between Earthlings and stellars (extraterrestrials) were those, in 1954, of the South African Elizabeth Klarer who mentions in her book *Beyond the Light Barrier* (1980) her contacts for 9 years until 1963, with the Centaurian Akon of the planet Meton, the smallest planet in the Alpha Centauri solar system where a Noor colony, one of the protohuman archetypes, has settled. The relationship between Elizabeth and Akon was consummated, from which their son Ayling was born. Klarer lived on Meton but had to return to Earth and left their son in Akon's custody. Ayling became an astrophysicist traveling through space with his father [43].

In 1957, another famous case was that of the Brazilian Antonio Villas-Boas who, after boarding a spacecraft, was subjected to medical examinations and sexual intercourse; Villas-Boas describes the experience in the following terms:

« A naked woman entered the room. She did not use a spoken language, but expressed her intentions clearly; [I] was suddenly caught up in an uncontrollable sexual excitement, which had never happened to me before.

[We had] sexual intercourse twice. She was making intermittent grunts that almost ruined everything, because they [made me] feel like I was in bed with an animal. The woman was beautiful, though not quite earthly.

She had silver-blond hair, a broad face with protruding cheekbones, a pointed chin and long blue bridled eyes... [I] felt that what [*the Small Greys*] were doing was using me as a stallion to improve their own herd. [17] »

In February 1989, kidnapped for 10 days, New Zealander Alec Newald reported in *Coevolution* (2011) that he had sex with a hybrid Havenite-human beautiful woman to develop the Havenites endangered species. The description fits Villas-Boas but in this case the woman could speak and did not growl like an animal [58].

British politician Simon Parkes openly discusses his relationship with an extraterrestrial lover whom he meets four times a year as well as the birth of his child whose name is Zarka [62].

Jacobs, in *The Threat* (1980), comments:

« Aliens almost always stared in the eyes of an abductee from a distance of a few inches or less and seemed to elicit...intense sexual arousal in men or women alike. By looking into people's eyes, these extraterrestrials also projected predetermined scenarios or movies into their minds. [40] »

Today, these same operations can be performed by stellars (extraterrestrials) who are able to transform emotions and generate feelings, of love, peace, hatred, anger or sexual arousal through direct and remote technology, targeting a single person or a whole group of people, in specific geographic areas, a neighborhood, a city or a country.

Jacobs continues:

« I was also puzzled as to why the abductees were

subjected to strange staging and testing procedures in

which they were playing a scenario with aliens or dis-

covering that they could use complex devices or per-

form tasks they did not recall learning... But one thing

was certain: the aliens engaged in an incalculable

number of abductions. A national survey conducted

by the *Roper Organization* in 1991 revealed an abduc-

tion program much larger than we had imagined.

[40] »

Hubrids conceived by sexual interaction by stellars (extraterrestrials)

and living with them on spaceships or in Earth bases, know their ori-

gins, but many hubrids, who are the results of breeding programs,

have no idea, because their memories and those of their parents are

suppressed.

They live on Earth in the same way as the rest of the population, but they generally exhibit higher-than-normal behaviors and abilities: clairvoyance, clairaudience, ability to heal, knowledge often beyond conventional sciences.

They are able to use their more advanced telepathic skills to create multiple levels of communication – from human to human or from human to stellars (extraterrestrials).

Natural hybridization between two extraterrestrial species is possible between close lineages: one of my contacts who was President D. Eisenhower's as well, the Five-Star General Rashell of Temmer, is a natural Antarian-Pleiadian hybrid: her mother Zoea of Temmer is a Pleiadian (Taygeta), and her father, Kartil, is an immigrant from Antares α Scorpii (Latinised to Alpha Scorpii).

Artificial hybridization is also used in programs of genetic mutations, between the humanoid race of the Lyra Constellation, the Lyrians, and the Zetas of the Zeta reticuli system (*Small Greys*). The new breed has the genetic superiority of both species.

ART. 32 - Bionic humans
Are the new technologies destroying our species? How do stellars (extraterrestrials) manage biology and technology?

32.1 – Bionic Humans

The fusion between biology and technology, the hybridization that was only a concept a few years ago, is increasingly part of our daily life: nomadic objects like the electronic bracelet, the RFID chip (Radio Frequency IDentification), more and more powerful mobile phones, smart lenses, GPS, MP3 players, home automation or augmented reality glasses are now attached to our daily life and the way we live.

Electronic implants technology such as myoelectric or bionic prostheses — the artificial heart *Carmat* implanted in a French patient [13], Isabelle Dinoire face transplant [26], Denis Chatelier two hands transplants [16], Jesse Sullivan two arms controlled by thought [74], the first pregnant man who gave birth to three children, Thomas Beatie, the GMOs of transgenic culture, hybrid cars — improve earthlings quality of life and longevity, but they all refer to the concept of hybridization becoming fully integrated to the Homo sapiens species.

32.2 – Extraterrestrial Management of Biology and Technology

Stellars (extraterrestrials) promote and develop both biology and technology simultaneously. They live in homes managed by very advanced artificial intelligence who are able to think, speak, feel and evolve independently and when they return home, they communicate with the house as they would with a pet. But in parallel, they built their house with their own hands, from A to Z, in the company of a group of friends, using natural materials made available to them free of charge in huge depots.

They also have ultra-sophisticated ships that they use to move around their planet as we use cars on Earth, but they build them themselves, including textiles that are handwoven.

Finally: they cultivate their garden and harvest by hand, they have a way of life close and respectful of the wild nature, but explore space at supraluminal speeds.

So the secret of balance is to respect the planet and wilderness, water, fauna and flora, and to use advanced technologies, but which have no impact on the environment.

ART. 33 - Terrestrial and extraterrestrial clones and cloning centers

Do human clones already exist? Do extraterrestrials have clones? Who are the clones and what are their roles?

Clones are common in the non-terrestrial world and it is also a growing industry on Earth. Exchanges and commercial operations take place daily, at a very high level between planets and species. Research and the production of cloning centers involve the creation of many hybrid forms as well as people entirely created from their DNA or who are genetically modified.

The treaties between extraterrestrial races and world governments have only endorsed a practice that had been developed for decades: Earthlings were abducted, locked up in storage cages in surface hideouts, or underground bases, tortured, raped, killed, used in laboratories, or for organ trafficking, sex trade, and slavery on Earth and with other planets; they also serve as nutritional resources: humans are not at the top of the food chain.

The hub of operations is in Antarctica, from which these multiple traffics can grow without any interferences from other nations.

Thousands of Earthlings who were kidnapped were saved by my extraterrestrial contacts during attacks of freighters that were delivering them to off planet locations. Some were so young that they did not speak yet or knew their name or their country of origin. They are now undergoing therapy in positive underground bases, or on allied spaceships, in care centers where their injuries and traumas are treated with healing technologies and medical beds (see ART. 56.4).

33.1 – Underground Bases and Cloning Centers

Scientific research laboratories, real cloning centers conducting important projects in genetic engineering, are integrated into vast underground bases (DUMBS) of which the largest are Dulce (NM) in the USA, and others in Bermuda, in China, in Russia, in Siberia, in Africa, in Australia, in New Zealand, in Afghanistan, in Iraq and in Antarctica, but also in Europe: Germany, Bosnia, Denmark, Spain, Greece, Italy, Norway, Sweden or in France.

The bases are located underground at different depths and in the seabed, often in isolated, difficult to access or unattractive locations. The different extraterrestrial races share geographical areas and gather together in a base according to their common interests; some are very active while others simply observe and collect samples.

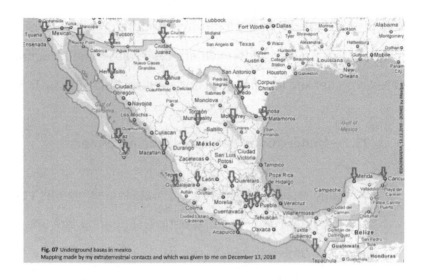

Fig. 07 Underground bases in mexico
Mapping made by my extraterrestrial contacts and which was given to me on December 13, 2018

Here is a map of the Mexican bases, which was drawn at my request, by my stellar (extraterrestrial) contacts and given to me on Thursday, December 13, 2018, at 6:21 p.m.

During my first two years of contact, I worked with my Mentor Zen on this issue of human trafficking and I presented to the Andromedan High Council, a set of directives to stop these practices. I required their commitment to help the races who use humans as a nutritional resource, to change their diet. They voted unanimously with the exception of one race and the first changes put in place were talks followed by the establishment of meat production from animal proteins produced in laboratories and 3D printing machines. The Urmahs (feline lineage) helped, because they use this method to no longer kill animals, but it is as difficult as trying to

convince an Earthling who is a big meat consumer, to become vegetarian or like asking a Lion to eat veggies. But they
started doing it and still are.

The center of underground operations was Dulce in New
Mexico, USA, before it was invaded by Allied Forces. These
autonomous bases, fully equipped and supplied, are gigantic
and are as extensive as the cities on the surface. They have
technologies unknown to the general public and are powe-
red by surface nuclear power plants.

They are located between one mile to several hundred miles
deep, below the large cities; Consider the mapping of cities
all over the planet, on the surface: the mapping is the same
underground. Each underground city can have up to 30 floors
that are accessible from specific surface entrances.

The bases are also accessible by spacecraft on the surface
(North Pole, South Pole, Mount Shasta and others) thanks to
entrances and tunnels so wide that two ships can fly together. These ships can pass from air to water instantly.

As in an international airport or hospital, each base has its
own entrances or access points and roads; they are accessible by car, and ultrafast elevators as well as an international

network of high-speed Maglev electromagnetic trains (745 ml/h – note that the Maglev speed record is 375 ml/h in Japan (2015) and 357 ml/h in France (2017). The networks cover the entire planet and connect the bases under any continent or ocean.

Each level is divided into research departments with specific laboratories. The first levels are used by human personnel and the deep levels for extraterrestrial personnel as well as for secret research.

33.2 - Underground Recreation and Entertainment Centers

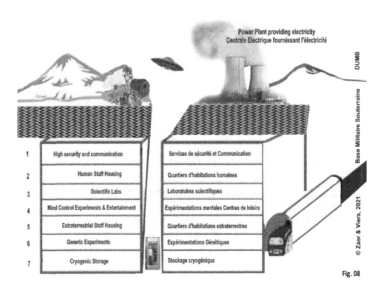

Fig. 08

The research laboratories (level -3) are linked to several underground hospitals open to a rich clientele for personal physical surgery and alterations.

But they are also coupled with huge entertainment and leisure centers giving access to paid event sessions for affluent people.

This clientele includes members of royal or influential families, celebrities, artists, athletes, musicians, models, writers, producers, actors, CEOs of multinationals and all kinds of people from various industries or science, but also presidents and all members of their governments, who are invited and quietly brought to attend themed entertainment or staging during which the participants interact with the clones and may indulge their most perverse inclinations. That's why Dulce's underground base, NM, USA was called *one of the largest brothels in this part of the galaxy* and hundreds of thousands of people were kept in captivity as sex slaves or ready to be shipped to off-planet colonies.

Powerful multinationals or transnational companies who are involved with governments and controlled by stellars (extra-terrestrials) are deeply involved in this field, for economic, scientific, industrial, territorial, financial and power purposes.

33.3 - Participants in underground sessions

These events involve the *production* that comes out of the laboratories, that is, terrestrial human clones or extraterrestrial human clones, and hybrid forms. The premises are therefore highly secured and controlled using advanced monitoring technology and brain wave/EEG control of all participants, guests, hybrids or clones.

This technology has the ability to read the brain to determine what their mind anticipates or speculates and to prevent attacks or dangers. Before participants leave the premises, people's brains are put into a state of trance to prevent them from clearly organizing their thoughts or remembering the existence of the cloning centers.

33.4 - Clone production and cloning techniques

These clones are made from their DNA, or DNA recovered from hair, skin or blood, and are *grown* in medical pods or artificial pockets filled with amniotic fluid and everything a fetus needs.

Then the transfer of a *soul* is carried out through copy-paste processes: the electromagnetic shell of consciousness in the brain is artificially moved to the body of a clone deemed compatible.

Various programming, synchronization, training, or game sessions then take place to prepare the clones for their future missions. Clones that look exactly like Homo sapiens are then used in multiple operations.

They are designed to live for a set period of time ranging from a few days to several hundred years and they have, like many products, an obsolescence date.

They can be put on sale in interstellar markets according to quality, durability, efficiency or beauty criteria that will vary their price up to nearly 1 million euros per unit.

33.5 – Six examples of clone use

-**Example 1.** a human clone made on Earth will be used for major public attacks and will be trained and programmed to destroy and kill.

Duration of obsolescence: from a few days to a few months,

-**Example 2.** a clone will be sent for military operations and infiltrate an enemy government.
Duration of obsolescence: several days to several years,

-**Example 3.** an army of clones will be sent to Mars as a group of workers, soldiers or sex slaves.
Duration of obsolescence: several years,

-**Example 4.** the clone of a magnificent extraterrestrial with perfect beauty criteria, made on earth, will serve as an escort or sex slave and will sell on the market nearly a million euros in High VIP clubs and sought after by billionaires.
Duration of obsolescence: according to fate.

-Example 5. a clone or group of extraterrestrial clones, manufactured on a spacecraft or other planet will be sent to Earth for political, military or consciousness-raising operations

Duration of obsolescence: a few days to hundreds of years,

-Example 6. clones of stars, film actors, and elected Presidents of some countries replace them in the event of failure or death.

Duration of obsolescence: the life of the person.

33.6 – Discrimination against clones

Stellars (extraterrestrials) reject conspiracies that have clones as their themes, because it is technically racist. Discrimination against cloned humans denies them the equality of fundamental rights to survival and protection from which any life, whatever it may be, can enjoy.

Stellars (extraterrestrials) consider them as full-fledged humans and consider them equal to any living person. Their DNA is identical to any human.

They receive specific software upgrades complementary to the programming integrated into their DNA that alter the reality they live in. They thus acquire new abilities and new perceptions of reality that you do not have.

ART. 34 – The Men in Black (MiBs)
Do MiBs really exist?

They are called MiBs, men in black because they wear black clothes, black Borsalino-type hats, black gloves, a trench coat with a black belt and they use black cars and black helicopters. Their missions are strategic, often involving intimidation or threats, and they work in pairs.

They are assigned to underground bases and during their missions, they are accompanied by doppelgangers or real metamorphic extra-terrestrials that are able to transform their appearance to appear human as well as by Earth soldiers. They use mental control or threat and fear as psychological weapons.

They are of two kinds:

1. Earthlings or human clones on Earth are controlled by elaborate combinations of confusion techniques, post-hypnotic suggestions, electromagnetic fields or chemicals temporarily impairing their perceptual and cognitive abilities,

2. people created synthetically and controlled by a group of extraterrestrials, who essentially work with different world governments. Synthetic MiBs are infiltrated into Earth societies in large numbers and the way to recognize them is similar to identifying an extraterrestrial metaphor: details do not match Earth's criteria. For example, they have no fingerprints and have a robotic behavior.

Published in May 2021, the testimony of Emily, a young American woman, whose father was part of the Air Force, describes them as follows:

> « It was unclear to my father and his team as to exactly who these individuals were, they speculated that they were quasi-government agents who harass, threaten or sometimes even assassinate UFO witnesses to keep them quiet about what they have seen. They thought they were possibly men working for unknown organizations, as well as various branches of government allegedly designed to protect secrets or perform other strange activities.

[He] said that they were very unusual, threatening and strangely behaved individuals...he described them as "Demonic supernaturals" with "dark skin and/or 'exotic' facial features", strange, shady and corrupted individuals who represent "experiences" that "don't seem to have occurred in the world of consensus reality.

...Extremely high-ranking military intelligence officers would refer to them as "THE SAUCER SPIES." My father told me many true stories about encounters that they experienced and my father and his team were 100 percent sure that these characters were "non-human".

They would suddenly appear out of thin air and disappear again just as quickly ... they knew [my father] had photographed them, but they just didn't seem to give a damn, many times they would do shady dealings in front of my dad and his teams.

They made transactions that seemed suspicious in front of my father and his team (see the photos of these characters passing information in broad daylight on the site referenced in the mediagraphy at the end of this book [55]).

For many years, even after retiring, my father was still harassed and watched by these entities.

...

[They began to be part of operations] after the extraordinary recovery of fallen airborne objects in the state of New Mexico, between July 4th and July 6, 1947, [The Roswell Crash] which caused the Chief of Staff of the Army Air Force-s Interplanetary Phenomena Unit, Scientific and Technical Branch, Counterintelligence Directorate to initiate a thorough investigation.

The special unit was formed in 1942 in response to two accidents in the Los Angeles area in late February 1942. The draft synthesis report begins - A 11:32 p.m. MST, July 3, 47, the radar stations in eastern Texas and White Sands Proving Ground, NM followed two unidentified aircraft until they both fell off radar.

Two crash sites were located near the WSPG. Site LZ-1 was located on a ranch near Corona, ca. 75 miles northwest of the town of Roswell. Site LZ-2 was located approximately 20 miles southeast of the town of Socorro, at latitude 33-40-31 and longitude 106-28-29.

The first-ever-known UFO crash retrieval case occurred in 1941 in Cape Girardeau, Missouri. This crash kicked off early reverse-engineering work, but it did not create a unified intelligence effort to exploit possible technological gains apart from the Manhattan project uses..

The debris from the primary of the 1947 crash 20 miles southeast of Socorro, New Mexico, was called ULAT-1 *Unidentified Lenticular Aerodyne Technology,* and it excited the metallurgists with its unheard-of tensile and shear strengths. The fusion nuclear (called neutronic at that time) engine use of heavy water and deuterium with an oddly arranged series of coils, magnets and electrodes strangely arranged – descriptions that resemble the cold fusion studies of today.

Harry Truman kept the technical briefing documents of September 24, 1947, for further study, pondering the challenges of creating and funding a secret organization before the CIA existed (although the Central Intelligence Group or CIG already existed)...

In April 1954, a group of senior officers from the American intelligence community and the Armed Forces gathered for one of the most secret and sensational briefings in history.

The topic was unidentified flying objects - not just a discussion about sightings, but how to recover crashed UFOs, where to ship the parts, and how to deal with the occupants.

For example, Extraterrestrial Entities Technology Recovery and Disposal, certain high-ranking military intelligence officers mapped out UFO crash retrieval scenarios with special attention given to press blackouts, body packaging, and live alien transport, isolation, and custody. [55] »

ART. 35 – The Borgs
Who and what are the Borgs?

The following is not an excerpt from Gene Roddenberry's *Science Fiction Star Trek* series [69], but it is what I was told in 2017, by Zen, my Mentor, as he was in the process of describing the different stellar (extraterrestrial) species he knew or was in contact with on a daily basis. At the time, an attempt to control a galactic zone was under way by crews of Borgs aboard a cube-shaped spaceship that suddenly appeared.

The Borg is a biohumanoid, android-like (male) or gynoid-like (female) robot, directed by state-of-the-art artificial intelligence in a permanent network. Their groups form a supra-individual whole, an egregore made up of their thoughts, intentions, strategies and all the data they collect; they are brought together in a sort of *hive* where the law of the community prevails, and to which the expression of personal identity is subject.

They are used by extraterrestrial controllers on Earth as MiBs. Their physical body consists of an organic base, a cloned human-like body fused with synthetic tissues and cybernetic implants. Implants allow them to communicate without using oral or written articulated languages and share information between them, at all levels instantly, to connect to other digital systems for example to the Internet or to infiltrate enemy offensive systems.

A Borg is most often equipped with appendages and tools to increase its field of competence and physical capabilities and repair the structures of a spacecraft.

The Borgs have no specific culture; Arts, music, and distractions are only useful because they are datasets they retrieve, but the emotions they generate are irrelevant to them.

When they colonize an area of space or a planet, they assimilate the most advanced species that possess knowledge, techniques or technologies that will allow them to expand the collective's global knowledge and they get rid of them.

They are perfectionists and they target the systematic assimilation of all the species that cross their path in order to acquire enough knowledge to progress and reach a state of total perfection.

ART. 36 - Transdimensional variants
What are extraterrestrial variants (Timeline variants)?

36.1 – Terrestrial Doppelganger

Doppelganger is a word derived from German folklore or Nordic mythology. It was popularized by linguists and philologists Jacob Grimm and Wilhelm Grimm who published tales known worldwide under the title « The Tales of the Grimm Brothers » whose most famous are *Snow White, Sleeping Beauty, Cinderella, Little Red Riding Hood, The Valiant Little Tailor, Hamelin's Flute Player.* [86].

The word *Doppelganger* means *lookalike, double of a living person,* an *alternative version,* a *reflection in the mirror* or, in many other cultures and beliefs, *another self* or *an alter ego.*

This term was taken up in literature from the 19th century to the present day by many authors such as Edgar Poe, Fyodor Dostoyevsky, Oscar Wilde, Agatha Christie; in science fiction as much as in art, painting, music, television series, or in films, it is presented in the form of evil doubles or robots.

36.2 – Stellar Variants (Extraterrestrials)

An extraterrestrial variant is the extraterrestrial physical version of the doppelgänger. These are multiple versions of the same person incarnated in multiple timelines or frequencies. These *versions* or *variants* look like twins, but unlike monozygotic twins (identical twins), which have the same genetic heritage and look exactly the same, these variants look like dizygotic twins (fraternal twins) that have different genes.

Their appearances are very similar, but many details differ from a physical as well as from a mental point of view. Some variants of the same person may be spiritual and positive and other ones negative and destructive. My contacts said:

« When you pilot a ship that has a warp engine you can fully fill it with the many versions of the same person. You can go from one timeline to another, cross the frequencies and abduct a person in a 3D or 5D timeline and make use of the person on a spaceship or another planet as a *copy* of the same person if the person is dead, or because she/he has a different mentality, or is spiritually more advanced. But you have to know that when you remove a variant from a family, you abduct the person who disappears leaving a void that can't be filled.

Sometimes the same younger *version* of a man will be used as *a sex stallion* and will be abducted from Earth to replace his older, less performing variant on an extraterrestrial spaceship. »

Zen, my extraterrestrial Mentor who was 148 years old in 2016, was confronted with this situation and at least three other younger versions of himself that he had to interact with after these men were abducted and brought over to his ship by the women in charge to use him for their intimate pleasure. They were abducted in the same place, in the same family, on the same 5D planet, but in different time lines and frequencies, and from *parallel* worlds.

The different versions of the same man (or the same woman), share the same *soul* and the same consciousness which gave rise to crazy situations that upset Zen, because a younger and impulsive version of him et controversial actions in place with negative consequences and he found it convenient to let him take the blame!

Chapter 4

REINCARNATION

FILLS UP WITH *SOULS*

ART. 37 – The *Soul*: Earth Concept
What is a *soul*? Is a *soul* immortal?

The stellar (extraterrestrial) concept of *soul* is inclusive. Ancient extraterrestrials who lived on Earth in ancient times are part of Earth actual concept of *soul*. Starting from debates on the immortality of the *soul or* eternal life, the journey of the concept describes the emergence of a vast interrogation on the identity and nature of man that has been prevalent for millennia.

Soul, or the word *néfesh* in Hebrew translated by *psyche* into Greek, *anima* in Latin, air, breath, the principle of life, *animus*, the seat of thought, but also of that of feelings and passions, concerns not a part of the human being, but the entire being. Many religious, philosophical, psychological, metaphysical, spiritual, or physical connotations describe the *soul* as an ontological entity distinct from the body, or an intrinsic part of the fundamental unity that constitutes the world.

In the philosophical sense it is the principle of sensitivity, in the metaphysical sense, its synonym *spirit*, is the *active* principle detached from the body that assures mental functions; in physics, it is of the same nature as the elementary particles of the universe which was defined at the beginning of the 20th century as having a *mass.*

What is the *soul?*

ART. 38 – the *soul* in prehistory
40,000 BC

It is difficult in the present state of research to detect at what moment the concept of *soul* emerged in its prehistoric origins, but it would be reductive to limit the way protohumans thought to *primitive mentality*, or to a form of *illogism*. The graphic representations, compositions and gestures of Rock Art, attest to an elaborate way of thinking, endowed with artistic refinement. The paleoanthropological and archaeological remains of the Neanderthals and Denisovians, their funerary rites, ornaments and offerings, seem to bear witness to a holistic perception of the universe and a belief based on an intimacy with the afterlife ; They were a way to keep a last visual memory of the person leaving them, a thank you or honor to the deceased, and a final farewell. But, just as the beliefs of the coming centuries, they may also have been a testimony in the conviction of a transition to another world.

Similar funerary rituals can be found in Homo sapiens cultures, which over the centuries gave rise to three major belief systems: animism, polytheism and monotheism.

    • Animism, considered today as the heir of the ancestral religions of humanity, is present among the indigenous peoples dispersed in more than 5000 groups (Aïnous, Bochi-mans, Dogons, Eskimos, Pygmies.) living on all continents; Belief is centered on a single god, and on higher spirits and deities. They attribute a soul distinct from the body to living beings, objects and natural elements, such as stones or wind.

• Polytheism is the belief in several or multiple gods, present in Mesopotamians, Egyptians, Greeks or Celts, Slavs, Hinduism, or pre-Columbian beliefs of Mesoamerica.

• Monotheist is centered on one single God: Judaism, Christianity and Islam.

ART. 39 – the *soul* in Hinduism
5000 years - 1500 years BC.

Hinduism is one of the oldest polytheistic religions that have brought the sublimation of the body through *yoga*, the illusion of the world, *maya*, the cycle of causes and effects related to existence, *karma;* Enlightenment or spiritual awakening, *nirvana*, as well as reincarnation, non-violence and vegetarianism.

The *soul,* or *ātman* आत मन according to the definitions of INRIA's Sanskrit Dictionary, can have several meanings: 1. the vital breath, the essential principle of life from which all living beings are organized, 2. the immutable essence of Being, beyond nature as we can grasp it, calm, unaffected by the movements of our inner nature, but supporting but not mingling with their respective evolution, 3. the transcendent and immanent Absolute, an ultimate principle without beginning or end, without birth or death, 4. the cosmic consciousness present in everything, the microcosmic form of the supreme self, as Brhad-Aranyaka Upanishad attests:

> « He who has realized and intimately known the
> Self, who has entered into this perilous and inac-
> cessible place [that is the body], is the creator of
> the universe, for he is the creator of all (everything
> is) his Self, and he is indeed again the Self (of

all). [80] »

The great originality of *ātman* in relation to the Greek and Western conceptions is that it has both personal and cosmic meanings: the individual *soul* emerges from the cycle of rebirth by merging into the cosmic, immanent and absolute *Soul*.

ART. 40 – The *soul* in Buddhism
6th century BC

The association of the words «*soul + Buddhism*» is an oxymoron, because the concepts of a creator god and that of a *soul* are absent. Different schools of Buddhism present a set of ethical values, or psychological, philosophical, cosmogonic, and cosmological theories, from the viewpoint of enlightenment, happiness, and liberation from suffering and ignorance.

The elements or events of the living are interdependent, from simple causes to effects and consequently, Buddhism advocates the ultimate emptiness of intrinsic realities and nothingness. By realizing it, and overcoming greed, anger, attachment and ignorance that hold him prisoner, the awakened human breaks the cycle of birth and death.

ART. 41 – The *soul* in Judaism
2nd century BC

Freed from the polytheism of the Mesopotamian myths, and from the Sumerian god Enki, or the Akkadian god Ea and those of the religion Ugarit, the king of the gods El (singular) or Elohim (plural) and his wife Asherah as well as their 60 divine children (Baal, Ashtarta, Shapshu..), Judaism is the first and therefore the oldest of the three great monotheistic religions.

It is based on a lunisolar calendar and the essential belief in a supreme Being, creator of the universe, which he rules by his providence by the use of the Jewish theology, law and cultural traditions.

The human *soul* in Judaism was born pure with an inclination to do good or evil and everyone uses free will to enjoy it in the way that is suitable for oneself. The *soul* is the very living being dependent on a visible physical body; it is mortal, but hopes for resurrection. Jewish mysticism considers that man possesses several *souls* in addition to the physical body: the spirit *(nêfesh)*, the breath, *anima (ru'ah),* the *soul, spiritus (neshamah),* life *(hayyah)* and union *(yehidah).*

ART. 42 – The soul *in Christianity*
1-4th century AD

Christianity, the second great monotheistic religion, presents the *soul* as the seat of consciousness. It is a principle of life, distinct from the body; it is immortal and immaterial. God makes the *soul* integrate a human body without the modalities of this integration being defined.

The *soul* is born tainted by original sin which can be redeemed individually by the sacrament of penance and reconciliation or collectively by the Passion and Resurrection of Christ. The individual as in Judaism enjoys full free will to decide to resort to it.

ART. 43 – The *soul* in Islam
6th century AD

The third great monotheistic religion, Islam advocates the separation of *soul* and body. The *soul* is breathed into the body 120 days after conception, leaves it at death and resurrects after God's judgment. Imam Abdullah, in his article *The Muslim Vision of the Soul*, states:

« God sends the angel to breathe the *soul* into the embryo in accordance with what has been narrated in an authentic account according to Companion Abd Allah ibn Massoud: « the Truest Messenger has told us that you are formed in the womb...then...you become a fetus...[and] the angel is sent to give the body a soul... »

« In spite of the accessibility of the body and the technological means, man still does not manage to detect all the secrets of the body...very difficult to reveal, even, inaccessible to human reason: « The *soul* belongs to the exclusive order of Our Lord and, in fact, from science, you have received very little. [1] »

ART. 44 – The *soul* of Greek Antiquity
470-322 BC

In Western philosophy, the *soul* was defined by many thinkers, the most famous of which are those of ancient Greece, Socrates, Plato and Aristotle, considered as the most illustrious that the world has known.

Socrates (in Greek Σωκράτης/ *Sōkrátēs*) is one of the inventors of moral philosophy and the father of Western philosophy. He left no writing and his knowledge was transmitted through the testimonies of his students who disclosed it by staging it in their own writing. It is therefore through the works of Plato, and his pupil Aristotle that the concept of *soul* developed.

Their works have, in turn, been studied and in an uninterrupted flow, the concept of *soul* has been conveyed to the present day thanks to the writing of an incalculable number of thinkers: Descartes (mathematician, physicist, philosopher), Hegel (philosopher), Kierkegaard (theologian, existentialist), Nietzsche (philosopher, philologist) or Freud, Jung, Lacan (psychiatrists, psychoanalysts) or Foucault (philosopher).

Plato (in Greek Πλάτων/ *Plátôn*) was a polymath, a poet, a musician, an athlete who received two awards at the Olympic Games. He formalized Socrates teachings and organized philosophy as a discipline, and a process of critical reflection and questioning about the world, knowledge and human existence. He gave birth to Platonism or Realism of ideas.

Plato devoted himself to the study of phenomena and to the descriptive knowledge of nature which he defended within the framework of the *theory of forms, theory of ideas* or *theory of intelligible forms* according to which abstract concepts, the notions or abstract ideas, really exist, are immutable and universal and form archetypes perceived by the sensory organs.

In his work, *Phaedon, or On the Immortality of the Soul*, the *soul* separates and survives death to find an intelligible eternal world.

> « Our soul is very similar to that which is divine, immortal, intelligible, simple, indissoluble, always the same, and always similar to itself, and...
>
> Our body resembles... to that which is human, mor-

tal, sensitive, composed, dissoluble, ever-changing, and never similar to itself;

...

The soul... in this state finds what is similar to itself... and is happy there, free from mistakes, from madness, from fears, from disordered love and from all the other human evils; and as the initiates say, the *soul* truly spends eternity in the company of gods... [65] »

Aristotle (in Greek Ἀριστοτέλης/ *Aristotelus*) joined Plato when he was only 17 years old and remained with him for twenty years. He was thus able to acquire a thorough knowledge of Platonic philosophy. But while Plato advocated ideas separated from essences, the dual separation between body and *soul*, Aristotle, seeks the principle of unicity and the indivisibility of being.

« What is, being, is what all particular beings participate in, without exception. Since nothing in itself can divide, increase or decrease it, it is unique, without beginning or end.

What is not, the imaginary entities, the past or the future, the multiple or what is divisible are outside of the intelligence, in the order of the opinion. [4] »

His *Treatise De l'Âme* is one of the first works in theory of knowledge that contributes to the foundation of modern psychology. It proposes a conception of being a *substance* and inaugurates the domains of *ontology* by questioning the meaning of the word *being,* and develops metaphysics as *the science of being as being.*

Aristotle designates the *soul* as *the prime entelechy*, the realization of that which is in power, by which the being meets perfection. It is both the body's form and essence.

> « Let us try to define what the soul is, and give it the most general notion possible... First of all, the substance is a particular aspect of all beings, and...it is necessary to distinguish, first: **matter**... then **form** and **species**... and third, the compound resulting from these first two elements. Matter is mere power; the species is perfect reality, the entelechy [which] must be understood in two ways: - the science which wants to know, or - the observation which knows.
>
> ...
>
> By this we see that it is not necessary to seek if the body and the soul are one and the same thing, no more than it is necessary to seek if the wax and the

figure it receives are identical... because One and Being having several meanings, the way in which one must [understand it] is the entelechy, perfect reality. [4] »

ART. 45 – The *soul* of the medieval West
5-15th century

Close to animism, the medieval clerical language borrows from Latin, the feminine word *anima* that transforms into *anema*, or *anme*
and *alme*, a dialectal variant, to become *âme (in French)*, the distinction between the living and the inert, or as Baschet explains it
in *Soul and body in the medieval West*, rather a *dynamic duality
between plurality and dualism*:

> « The medieval theology offers hundreds of occur-
> rences of the following statement, which can be
> held to be the central axis of its conceptions: the
> human being is formed by the conjunction of a
> body, fleshly and perishable, and a soul, spiritual
> entity, incorporeal and immortal. Or what will be
> called a dual but not necessarily dualistic, design.
> [7] »

In the 13th century, the definition of the *soul* was extended to the
spiritual principle of man; the writer Girart d'Amiens in his verse
novel *Escanor* (1280) presents it as one of the two principles com-
posing man: the body and the *soul*. [21]

ART. 46 – The *Soul* in Philosophy
16th–17th century

In the 16th century, the concept or idea of *soul* refers to a principle that animates the body of a living human, animal or plant; in his work *Histoire Universelle*, Théodore Agrippa d'Aubigné, a provocative writer-controversist and baroque poet — whose granddaughter, Françoise d'Aubigné, became the Marquise de Maintenon, Louis XIV's wife — extended this principle to *the sensitive soul (of animals)* and to *the vegetative soul in plants.* [22]"

For his part, René Descartes, considered as one of the founders of modern philosophy and author of the *cogito ergo sum* «I think so I am» in the *Discourse of the Method and Metaphysical Meditations*, stresses the distinction between body and *soul*-thought, the manifestation of the individual as a thinking being that must be demonstrated by reason and not, he says, by belief:

> «I knew by this that I was a substance whose whole essence or nature is only to think, and which in order to be needs no place or depends on any material thing; so that this self, that is to say the soul, by which I am what I am, is entirely distinct from the body :

To the Deans and Doctors of the Sacred Faculty of Theology - Gentlemen, I have always considered that the two questions of God and of the soul were (...) the main ones which must rather be demonstrated by the reasons of Philosophy, rather than by [the beliefs] of Theology. [24] »

The definition of the word *soul* evolved leading to the emergence of a living principle, and testifies to successive contradictory paradigms; Is it vain to ask the question of what the *soul* is?

The meaning of the word or the nature of what the *soul* is become elusive in the light of the often discordant perspectives, for the question is intrinsic to the discourse; it is the principle of the predicate inherent in the subject «Praedicatum inest subjecto», stated by Gottfried W. Leibniz, polymath, mathematician and philosopher, or Aristotle's disillusioned observation emphasizing it was futile to try to ask, because it would be asking oneself « *if the wax and the figure it receives are identical.* [4] ».

ART. 47 – The *Soul* of the Age of Enlightenment
17th–18th century

From 1715 to 1793, from Louis XIV to Louis XVI and Marie-Antoinette of Habsburg-Lorraine, it was in the context of France confronted with serious economic and social problems that intellectual changes took place, at the crossroads between religion and science, or belief and logic. During this period, which was a major societal pivot, the pre-eminence of thought and critical thinking enlightened darkness and ignorance. The *Enlightenment movement,* also known as *the Age of Enlightenment*, is philosophical, literary, cultural and scientific and aims at overcoming obscurantism through knowledge.

The emergence of Copernicus (16th century) heliocentric model, later supported by Galileo during the 17th century, came from his experiments with his astronomical telescope, the theory of universal gravitation and the publication in 1687 of *Philosophiae naturalis principia mathematica, Mathematical Principles of Natural Philosophy*, Isaac Newton's masterpiece, will allow the development of a mathematical formalism and logic yet unknown.

They will question the ideas developed in the Middle Ages, the renewal and reorganization of knowledge. Philosophers and thinkers, by encouraging science through intellectual exchange, advanced knowledge and give rise to an unprecedented reflection on the nature of the human being and the immateriality or immortality of the *soul.*

The elements that illustrate this period are essentially: 1. reason and rational reflection, 2. the rejection of Christian ideology, 3. the autonomy of people capable of reasoning by itself.

Drawing closer to the world of printing, thinkers compile a synthesis of knowledge and the first French encyclopedia is born under the title *Encyclopédie ou Dictionnaire raisonné des sciences, des arts et des métiers;* the publication conducted by encyclopedists under the direction of Denis Diderot and Jean Le Rond d'Alembert is set in this context of the emergence of a new form of thought and Newton's theories disseminated by Voltaire.

The definition of the *soul* given in the first volume of the *Encyclo-*

pedia is based on the writings of the theologian Abbé Yvon, who had presented a history of the metaphysical doctrines of the *soul.*

A M E

A M E 327

AME, f. f. *Ord. Encycl. Entend. Raif. Philof. ou Sciences des Esprits, de Dieu, des Anges, de l'Ame.* On entend par *ame* un principe doüé de connoissance & de sentiment. Il se présente ici plusieurs questions à discuter : 1°. quelle est son origine : 2°. quelle est sa nature : 3°. quelle est sa destinée : 4°. quels sont les êtres en qui elle réside.

Il y a eu une foule d'opinions sur son origine; & cette matiere a été extrèmement agitée dans l'antiquité, tant payenne que chrétienne. Il ne peut y avoir que deux manieres d'envisager l'*ame*, ou comme une qualité, ou comme une substance. Ceux qui pensoient qu'elle n'étoit qu'une pure qualité; comme Epicure, Dicéarchus, Aristoxène, Asclepiade & Galien, croyoient & devoient nécessairement croire qu'elle étoit anéantie à la mort. Mais la plus grande partie des Philosophes ont pensé que l'*ame* étoit une substance. Tous ceux qui étoient de cette

opinion, ont soutenu unanimement qu'elle n'étoit qu'une partie séparée d'un tout, que Dieu étoit cé tout, & que l'*ame* devoit enfin s'y reunir par voie de réfusion. Mais ils différoient entr'eux sur la nature de ce tout; les uns soutenant qu'il n'y avoit dans la nature qu'une seule substance, les autres prétendant qu'il y en avoit deux. Ceux qui soutenoient qu'il n'y avoit qu'une seule substance universelle, étoient de vrais athées : leurs sentimens & ceux des Spinosistes modernes sont les mêmes; & Spinosa sans doute a puisé ses erreurs dans cette source corrompue de l'antiquité. Ceux qui soutenoient qu'il y avoit dans la nature deux substances générales, Dieu & la matiere, concluoient en conséquence de cet axiome fameux, *de rien rien*, que l'une & l'autre étoient éternelles

Fig. 10

[*Transcript:* SOUL,... Philosophy, Sciences of Spirits, of God, of Angels, of the Soul. By *soul* we mean a principle endowed with knowledge and feeling. There are several questions to be discussed here: 1° what is its origin; 2° what is its nature; 3° what is its destiny; 4° what are the beings in whom it resides.

There have been many opinions about its origin and this matter has been extremely agitated in both pagan and Christian antiquity. There can be only two ways of considering the *soul*, or as a quality, or as a substance. Those who thought that it was only pure quality as Epicurus, Dicearque, Aristoxenus, Asclepiaede and Galien, believed and must necessarily believe that it was annihilated at death. But most of the philosophers thought the *soul* was a substance. All those who were of this opinion unanimously maintained that it was only a separate part of a whole, that God was that whole, and that the soul should finally meet there... But they differed among themselves on the nature of this whole; some argued that there was only one substance in nature, while others argued that there were two. Those who maintained that there was only one universal substance were true atheists: their feelings and those of modern spinozists are the same. And Spinoza no doubt drew these errors from this corrupt source of antiquity. Those who maintained that there were in nature two general substances, God and matter, conclude as a result of this famous axiom, of nothing, that both were eternal.]

This publication and the connection that Diderot makes in some of his writings with scientific discoveries will give rise to the brand new *science of man* at the heart of which the materialistic and mechanistic theories of time, such as that defended by Julien Ofray de La Mettrie in *L'Homme machine* will rise in power.

During a fever attack, La Mettrie, who had studied medicine, noticed the action of accelerated circulation on his thought; he deduces that what he calls *spirit* or *soul*, must be considered as a continuation of the sophisticated organization of matter in the brain:

« What is this generation, this birth of Ideas, that produces the taste of Nature and the search for the True? How to paint this Act of the Will, or of the Memory, by which the Soul reproduces itself in some way, by attaching an idea to another similar trace, so that from their likeness and...from their union, a third is born; because admire the productions of Nature. Such is its uniformity that they are almost all made in the same way. [49] »

Debates on ideas are developing, knowledge is growing and spreading, particularly in connection with the press, the number of bookshops is increasing and the sale of religious books is decreasing in favor of books on science, history and philosophy. In their private rooms, the women of the nobility and the upper bourgeoisie organize receptions where they invited great thinkers of the time, as described by Zaor & Viera:

« In this context of questioning the political regime, Olympe de Gouges became the figurehead of a movement of women who wanted to be equal to men. She publishes *the Declaration of the Rights of Women and Citizens*...with the hope of transforming men and other women's thoughts...the most reckless were politicized. They used to meet and run from meetings to private salons, demanding their rights, their full place in civil and political life, the right to divorce, their share of inheritance, their name on a deed of property, a better life. They comforted each other in the illusion that they would soon see the birth of a society that would listen to them, where their rights would finally be recognized. Ah! Freedom! Silk, power and gold! It was the time of great hope. [84] »

Thinkers in search of the truth in the universe keep recalling the reasons for distancing themselves from metaphysics. They reject the intolerance of the debates on God or the *soul and* postulate the marginalization of knowledge that still is a matter of faith, of irrational adherence or of intuition and superstition.

The philosopher Emmanuel Kant, in *La Critique de la Raison Pure* analyzes in a rational way the different faculties of the mind and the nature of the soul:

« 1° The soul is a substance − 2° *Simple*, as to its quality − 3° Numerically identical, that is to say unity (non-plurality), as to the different times when it exists − 4° Related to possible objects in space.

It is from these elements that all the concepts of pure psychology result; it is enough to bring them together, without any other principle to recognize. This substance, considered only as an object of an inner sense, gives the concept of *immateriality;* as a simple substance, that of incorruptibility; its identity, as intellectual substance, gives *personality*; and the three things together constitute *spirituality*. Its relationship to objects in space gives commerce with bodies. It therefore represents the thinking substance as the principle of life in matter, that is, as a soul *(anima)*, and as the principle of *animality*. [41] »

Kant rejects metaphysics as science for its experiential nature, not objective, nor based on absolute principles, and formalizes the substitution of anthropology for the metaphysics that characterizes the Age of Enlightenment. What is rejected, it seems, is not so much the domain of metaphysics properly speaking, as the scientific status to which it claims by demonstrating truths susceptible of universal acceptance.

In the sciences as well as in philosophy, Jean Le Rond d'Alembert, mathematician, physicist and philosopher, who participated in the composition of the *Encyclopedia* with Diderot incorporates the tradition of Cartesian reason to Newtonian conceptions, opening the way to modern scientific rationalism.

It is in this context of the metamorphosis of thought that philosophers are led to take sides in the name of the values they defend in political and social problems such as the development of liberalism in the economy, the emancipation of women, the emancipation of slaves, the development of political freedoms, the fight against censorship, the fight for religious tolerance. Important discussions take place, posed by philosophers as the necessity for human beings to find individual happiness and to erase inequalities by highlighting the progress allowed by civilization, rationalism and science. Zaor & Viera, *Cosmic Transmutation*, chapter *10h* reproduced here in full [84]:

« Execution by beheading was institutionalized when the great thinkers of the revolution developed the concept of equal rights, including equality in death. In the 1789's, a group of revolutionaries, the military surgeon Antoine Louis, perpetual secretary of the Academy of Surgery, the architect

Giraud, the carpenter Guidon, the *maker,* Tobias Schmidt, harpsichord and pianoforte maker who made instruments in his workshop at the Cour du Commerce, rue Saint-André-des-Arts, in the scents of linden wood and spruce, and a Master-Executioner Charles-Henri Sanson, without properly measuring the short- and long-term cause-and-effect relationships, under the direction of Dr. Joseph Ignace Guillotin, would become the designers, owners and builders of revolutionary technology.

Notwithstanding their respect or empathy for humanity, these six men, will think, design, build, test and institutionalize a machine that they intended to guarantee equality in the execution of the death penalty to give birth one day, they hoped for a future in which the death penalty would one day, be abolished.

As their paths crossed, one of them devoted himself to writing the first great texts on which the future of his fellow citizens would rest, and proposed a new penal law.

In order that the people might be taken into account as a whole and become a power in their own right, behavior, mentality, laws especially could no longer treat the rich and the aristocrats kindly and trample the poor, the peasants like animals.

Equality was to be established not only from a social, cultural and political point of view, but also through a criminal stance. But the big question he asked was: « how to ensure that the death penalty, the execution of prisoners who were condemned, is applied equally for the rich and for the poor, without discrimination? ».

At first, this discreet anatomy enthusiast, who did not tolerate injustice or the terrible tortures inflicted on the condemned, began by launching a petition in which he made change the modalities of the voting system: an equal number of deputies and representatives of the nobility or clergy and votes per head.

The particular point of the laws on which he was

working was a decree on capital punishment and its application. How do we define it? That is to say, on what criteria should the penal system sentence an individual to the death penalty? Should it be institutionalized and what means should be used to ensure that death is equal for all?

The pyre, the drowning, the gallows, the wheel, the mutilation, the dislocation of the skeleton, the distension of the limbs, the pincers, the burning fire, the boiling oil, the molten lead: the ingenuity of the application of punishment was as rich as the crual imagination of the human beings who invented them and the judges who decided it.

The nobles were quick to die by decapitation with a sword, the commoners with an axe, the regicides and the state criminals were quartered, the heretics burned at the stake, the thieves beaten or hung, the counterfeiters boiled alive in a cauldron. [87]

In the case of the sword or the axe, the neck had

to be cut several times before the head fell and the tortures could last for hours, before the horrified eyes of the next condemned who waited their turn.

But if the law convict,

Justice does not seek revenge.

Echafaud, d'après une gravure ancienne
(xvᵉ s.).   Fig. 12

According to the principle of equality of rights laid down in Article 1 of the Declaration of Human and Citizen's Rights, « *Men are born and remain free and equal in rights* » and if equality did not extend to capital punishment, this principle could not prevail in criminal law. The law had to be **reformed**.

Guillotin therefore introduced a bill to institutionalize the death penalty and, after discussing it with his fellow surgeon, a quicker killing that would replace all other forms of execution.

Out of humanism, probably moved by the pain of the victims, so that they would not have to endure these atrocities and strong of his oath of Hippocrates, Doctor Joseph, decided one day, to put an end to these humiliating practices and an end to the butchery. He began to think about a process that was fairer, less painful, and therefore more effective; a more prompt means, which could give death without causing these numerous tortures to the condemned.

A mechanical process.

We would use a mechanical force instead of human force. The same force, which would no longer depend on the Executioner's state of health or on a heavy drinking the day before, but which would be direct without repeating and without mistakes. Artisanal techniques could no longer be used and the execution project was managed as a logistics project.

Rationality, economy of means, economy of pain, economy of dignity, standardization and legalization of the death penalty. Equality for all. Equality in death.

In the context of the technical development that continued its course from Florence in the 14th century and inspired by a machine that already existed in Germany, Italy, Scotland and Great Britain, the *thinking* part of the group drew the first plans and a first prototype was built.

On a Friday afternoon, the machine was assembled in the Cour du Commerce in Paris and the first functional and clinical trials were carried out on chickens, sheep and calves, dead and alive, to define the different stages of death and the effects of decapitation; all worked together to refine the details and efficiency of the construction, and the Public Executioner gave his opinion to address the sensitive questions of the procedure, of the pain, of the difficulties that would be encountered during the actual execution.

It was his job, he would run the machine in the field.

Then the medical, ethical, ethical issues of death

were studied. From their perspectives, from the knowledge and practices at the time of invention, death seemed softer and quicker.

The law was then passed and promoted, the machine built on the line and sent to all the French departments where it stopped being used in 1977.

Sometimes the line of demarcation between wanting to do the good of humanity and dragging the human being towards its loss, is tenuous.

Each of us has a choice to cross that line. Whether we like it or not, our actions, however insignificant they may be, spread on our consciences and on all that lives, like mechanical waves on the surface of water because everything in the universe is interconnected.

This thought was not carried out at the time and the success of the machine was beyond the control of its designers. Executions accelerated and took place in the tens of thousands in Paris and throughout France... In Paris alone, 3,000 people will lose their heads in two years: 1,500 people a year, and more than four people a day.

Faced with these excesses, Dr. Guillotin then fought for the abolition of the institutional death penalty, especially since the famous machine now bore his name. He worked on the Declaration of Human Rights and established the first national public health program in France.

Until his death, he will bitterly regret having participated in the invention of the machine and will be haunted by the terrible consequences that persisted for centuries.

The public Executioner Charles-Henri Sanson continued his work, proud of his lineage, at the edge of throwing up his guts, whenever he dropped the blade. He also worked for the abolition of the death penalty.

Guillotine.

Fig. 13

The *Bois de Justice* was first called *Louisette* or *Louison* after the name of the surgeon Antoine Louis. It was given all kinds of nicknames: *big national razor, silent mill, cutter.* But the crowd, the history and the great memory of humanity will prefer to call it *guillotine.* »

Within the framework of what concerns us, the soul, the reason of the philosophers of the Enlightenment with emancipatory vocation, has sunk into unprecedented forms of violence and ruthless domination, instead of a fully human commitment to respect for the rights of humanity.

ART. 48 – The *Soul* in Psychology
19-21ème siècle

The 19th century discovers the philosophy of Friedrich Nietzsche, philosopher, poet and writer who brings together the *soul* and the body as the *soul's master:* « Body I am entirely, and nothing else, and soul is only a word for something in the body. [59] »

Nietzsche explains that, since the body is made up of desires, impulses, instincts and unconscious wills directing our thoughts, they are only the products of organic impulses. There is no autonomous *soul* in the body. In *Thus spoke Zarathustra*:

> "Behind your thoughts and feelings, my brother,
> there stands a powerful master, an unknown guide
> – called Self. In your body it dwells, it is your body."

The journey of Zarathustra among men marks the starting point of the thought of the rise of a **superman**: God is dead and since he can no longer be the finality of the human will, humanity must set itself an immanent goal passing through its own surpassing.

> « Companions are what the creator seeks, not corpses, herds or believers. Creators like him are

what the creator is looking for, those who put new values on new tables. »

In analytical psychology, the *soul*, or *psyche* refers to the inner life and the unconscious depths of being, unveiled in the 19th century, by three theorists, authors and pioneers: Freud, Jung and Lacan.

All three had gathered their knowledge according to a transdisciplinary approach, mythology, alchemy, Taoism, linguistics, mathematics... and visualized the human psyche with several components; according to Jung, it is structured in five areas: 1. Me/Ego 2. consciousness 3. personal unconscious (shadow + anima/*animus)*, 4. collective unconscious, 5. a part of the collective unconscious that can never become conscious.

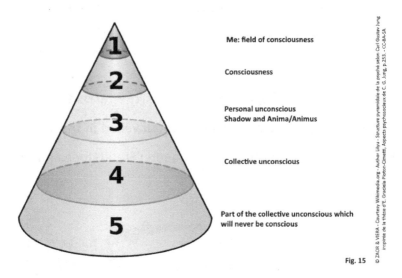

Me: field of consciousness

Consciousness

Personal unconscious
Shadow and Anima/Animus

Collective unconscious

Part of the collective unconscious which
will never be conscious

Fig. 15

Sigmund Freud, neurologist, founder of psychoanalysis, found the unconscious by limiting himself to dreams, witticisms, lapses, missed acts or pathological and neurotic behaviors.

While **Carl Gustav Jung**, psychiatrist, founder of analytical psychology, and formal friend and disciple of Freud who became his rival, stresses the link between the structure of the *psyche-soul* and its cultural manifestations. To transgress the conscious barrier, like Freud, he explores dreams, but also visions, phantasms, alchemical engravings-conscious projections of unconscious materials and the myths which, according to his interpretation, are representations of archetypes. (The *myths* according to extraterrestrials are a forgotten reality, not myths. They represent the distorted memory of a forgotten terrestrial human reality).

Jacques Lacan, psychiatrist and psychoanalyst, founder of Lacanism, takes over all Freudian concepts, and does research in linguistic structuralism and linguistics. He draws on theology, cybernetics, ethnology and linguistics to enrich psychoanalysis. It also reiterates the idea that the psychic life of each one is to act for the satisfaction of his differences, and invites to recognize that in the paranoid for example his illusions have no less consistency and interest than the conventionally recognized truths.

ART. 49 – The soul of atomists and physicists
20-21st Century

Atomism is a philosophical current that has its roots in the Hindu philosophy of the VI-6th c. BC. It combines the real with the non-being, which has as much reality as the being. For Atomists the *soul* is composed of atoms like any object and a conception of a consubstantial universe, composed of matter and void, the same fundamental unified *substance.* This perception of being-not-being, has also passed through the centuries to the present day to be founded in the West, in the 5th century BC, by Leucippe and his disciple Democritus d'Abdere, until the development of physics, nuclear fission and the research of the Higgs boson, the God particle.

The existence of the elementary particle was confirmed experimentally by the ATLAS and CMS experiments at the CERN large hadron collider (particle accelerator) in Geneva and led to the awarding of the Nobel Prize in Physics to François Englert and Peter W. Higgs in 2013 [35]; it explains why some particles have a mass and others do not.

HIGGS ENGLERT

Fig. 16

The simultaneous presence of a mass and a lack of certain particles could perhaps explain the theological, philosophical or psychological concepts of the *soul* separated from the body or, on the contrary, fused with the body, which has haunted human thought since the dawn of time. The human eye cannot see the atom, but could it be detected by some sensitive abilities beyond the known or sensory perceptions?

Some even deliberated on the « weight of the soul », as if it were a part of the body, which in 2003 became the title of a film by Alejandro González Iñárritu, entitled *21 grams* [39].

Why should the *soul* weigh precisely 21 grams?

The title of the film refers to the research on the *substance* of the *soul* evoked by philosophers and by the American physician Dun MacDougall. McDougall believes that if the soul is or has substance, unless there is a break in the mechanics of physics, this substance can only exist as a body occupying space, and therefore it has a mass that should be measurable.

This mass, wrongly called *soul weight*, became the theory of 21 grams, after being published in 1907 and entitled *Hypothesis Concerning Soul Substance Together With Experimental Evidence of the Existence of Such Substance* — *by the* Journal of the American Society for Psychical Research. McDougall raises the issue in these terms:

> « If personal continuity after bodily death is a fact, if the psychic functions continue to exist as individuality or separate personality after the death of the brain and body, such a personality can exist only as a body occupying space, unless — but it is difficult for me to imagine it because it would be a breach in the continuity of nature — that the relations between

space, and the notions of space in our consciousness, established in our consciousness, by heredity
and experience, are completely erased at death and
that a new set of relationships is suddenly integrated
into the continuity of personality.

It is unthinkable that personality and consciousness
perpetuating personal identity exist and have an
existing, without occupying space.

It is impossible to represent in thought that which
occupies no space, as having personality, for it would
be equivalent to that *nothing* has become or was something, that emptiness has personality, that space
itself is more than space...these are just absurd
contradictions.

Since it is therefore necessary for the continuation of
conscious life and personal identity after death, that
they must have as a basis what occupies space or
substance, the question then arises of the weight of
this substance; is it ponderable? [51] »

According to his hypothesis at the time of death, the *soul* would escape from the human body, which would be *relieved* of this weight.
MacDougall advances the figure of 21 grams after having carried
out a series of weighing on six moribund humans later deceased, of

which only one shows a mass difference of about 21 grams; he repeated his experience on about fifteen dogs, without showing any
difference in their case.

These results could never be confirmed and MacDougall's methods
were widely criticized and criticized for their lack of scientific rigor.

The term *weight* that McDougall uses, which refers to the gravity
force due to the gravitational pull of the Earth, could be replaced
by the words *volume* or *density [ρ]* or *density of mass*, the weight
of the *soul* then becoming the density of the *soul*, and by extension, the frequency or spectral power density whose mathematical
function would allow the possibility of a representation of the frequency distribution of a *signal* core power, according to a set of frequencies. These suggestions are only vague interpretations on my
part, which would hardly be supported at this point, given the separation that still exists today, on Earth, between physics and philosophy; I think, however, that some philosophical assumptions could
be interpreted scientifically.

Chapter 5

POLYPTYCH OF REINCARNATION

ART. 50 – Reincarnation: Definitions
What is reincarnation?

Incarnation, and indeed reincarnation, from Latin *incarnatus* or *incarno* | taking or clothing a body of flesh | means the integration of a spirit into the flesh, in a physical form. It is synonymous with *metempsychosis, metensomatosis, transubstantiation, transmutation or transmigration, cosmic* and *universal palingenesis, soteriology, eternal return, karma* or *the samsaric wheel.*

• Metempsychosis •

refers to a set of cyclic transformative phases of post-mortem survival by which an immaterial principle *soul, vital substance, consciousness*, would perform successive transitions from one life to the next.

• Metensomatosis •

is the passage of the *spiritual body* into a new body after physiological death; the spiritual body would move to a new physical existence in the tangible world and would take another human, animal, vegetable, mineral or spiritistic form.

• Transubstantiation •

in anatomy, it means the replacement of a tissue by elements of another species. In psychology it is a mental transfer by which something mundane becomes exceptional, sacred and of the order of the divine.

• Transmutation and transmigration •

qualify the molting of one substance into another. In nuclear physics, it is the transformation of a chemical element by a modification of the atomic nucleus. The term *transmutation* is also used in alchemy to describe the transformation of one substance into another, or even an element into another (water, earth, fire and air) and the transmutation of base metals (copper, iron, tin, lead, mercury) into noble metals (gold, silver).

• Cosmic or universal palingenesis •

defines the exchange, assimilation or redistribution and therefore the transformation of the natural components of life: plants feed on minerals, animals feed on plants, humans feed on animals and by breathing, all that is alive assimilates germs and dust.

• Soteriology •

relates to the theology of soul salvation which occupies an important place in many ancient religions and philosophies, focused on the immortality of the soul and its migration after death into a paradise or hell according to the merits of each.

• karma and the samsaric wheel •

is related to the *Eternal Return,* a rebirth of the *soul, a* metamorphosis, migration or *transmigration* after death, and a cyclical process in a loop, which continues until the soul is freed from materiality, the uninterrupted chain of causes and effects or the samsaric wheel of birth and death. The *soul* would therefore pass through as many reincarnations as necessary to free itself from them and to evolve towards a state of *being*, accomplished or realized.

ART. 51 – Beliefs and reincarnation
Does life end definitively once our physical body dies? Does human consciousness survive after death? **Is death the end of everything?** Where does the *soul* go after death?

In 2003, a survey of beliefs shows that 39% of French people think that there is nothing after death, 33% assume that there is something, without being able to say what it is exactly. 16% say they believe in immortality, 6% in reincarnation and 4% in the resurrection of the body. [68]

Modernity - through advances in scientific knowledge, technological development, the process of rationalization, individualism and pragmatism - has certainly seriously undermined religious dogmas, but in the end it did little to begin with the human need – justified or not – to believe.

This is why we are witnessing the development of a new *extraterrestrial religiosity,* veneration à la carte where everyone freely makes his choice in the shopping galleries of interstellar races, especially non-human species, *reptilian* or *small grey types.*

The current prevailing idea installed at the heart of the belief in reincarnation, has axiomatized under various definitions around a central theoretical or dogmatic unanimity, that of successive life schools where the *soul* progresses step by step in order to reach the full spiritual realization and the free choice of a future incarnation.

But the concept of reincarnation or an extension of dematerialized life to an invisible world is not new and it did not appear at a precise moment in the history of humanity; it has always been present, because it is linked to death.

Since the dawn of humanity, human beings have always asked themselves the question of the mystery of death and what follows it. Reincarnation is part of the ancestral beliefs that seem to answer the questions, « what happens after death? » « Does life end definitively once our physical body dies? » , « is death the end of everything? »

• 51.1 – Aboriginal India

Long before the development of Hinduism, when religions did not yet exist, the *transmigration of souls* and the need to lead a pure life so as not to be reborn in an animal's body, already existed in animist or shamanic practices of prehistoric and Aboriginal India. Antic remains seem to testify to the importance of a belief based on an *intimacy* of the afterlife for ancestral peoples. They, like those who will follow, bear witness to their convictions that there was a transition and a passage to an invisible world after the physical death.

Over time, Aboriginal notions will spread over a very large territory, influencing and marking with their weight, the theories on reincarnation.

• 51.2 – Hinduism

The sacred texts are revealing developments in this field, in particular the Bhagavad-Gita, one of the fundamental writings of Hinduism;

Krishna, in his teaching, explains to Arjuna what reincarnation is:

« As the incarnate soul passes through this body from childhood to youth to old age, the soul takes a new body to death. The realized soul does not disturb such a change. [6] »

« As a person puts on new clothes...the soul accepts new material bodies, giving the old useless. [6] »

Metempsychosis, although not universally recognized, is a central belief of Hinduism. Some of the thousand cases recorded in the country have become famous as that of Shanti Devi a little girl who in the 1930s, declared at school that her home was not her home, that she was a Brahmin woman, born in Mathura, and had died a few days after giving birth to a child.

Questioned by one of her teachers and the Principal of the school, she spoke in the Mathura dialect and revealed that her husband was a merchant and his name was Kedar Nath. After research, the Principal located a merchant in Mathura who had lost his wife, Lugdi Devi, nine years earlier, ten days after giving birth to a son.

The story of Shanti became so popular throughout India that it was brought to the attention of Mahatma Gandhi who came to visit her and moved by her suffering in the face of the misunderstanding that surrounded her, Gandhi persuaded her parents to submit her to a committee of inquiry. Taken to her 'hometown', the child demonstrated that she was able to find her home, recognize her husband, her former neighbors, and the parents of her previous life. The 1936 commission report concluded that Shanti Devi was the reincarnation of Lugdi Devi. [50]

Another case is that of an eight-year-old boy, Chandraveer Shankhwar, *alias* Chotu, who claims to be the reincarnation of a thirteen-year-old teenager, Rohit Kumar, who drowned on May 4th, 2013, while bathing in a canal in Nagla Salehi a village near the city of Manipuri, in the state of Uttar Pradesh, in Northern India.

Chotu identified his mother and sister without hesitation and then embarked on a narrative of his life as Rohit, providing such stunning details and anecdotes that his story made the headlines. [71]

The belief in reincarnation exerts an undeniable influence on Indian culture. However it is not uniformly present throughout the country; it varies significantly across regions, populations and social groups. Ramana Maharshi, at the Ahram in Tiruvannāmalai, in the south of India, one of the greatest thinkers whose teachings are centered on non-duality, the notion of Self and the question *Who am I?* stated that « one should not believe that any individual ego can be reborn after death, the soul being neither the self, nor the ego, nor the personality, nor the intellect. »

• 51.3 – Buddhism

Buddhists unanimously believe in reincarnation, although this doctrine does not appear expressly — on the contrary — in the primitive Teaching held to have been directly proclaimed by the Buddha Siddhartha Gautama, from which God and the *soul* are absent.

Nevertheless, the concept of *reincarnation* or *rebirth* and the fundamental notion of karma abound as a continuity, the *samsāra*, ससर Sanskrit term meaning "all that circulates", the cycles of life that follow one after the other according to the law of causality.

Some Buddhist schools, such as that of the Gelugpa Yellow Hats, one of the four great schools of Tibetan Buddhism, refer to *reincarnation* as *metensomatosis*, a slip, a « displacement of the spiritual body » towards a new physical existence in the tangible world.

The 14th and current Dalai Lama, birth name Lhamo Dhondup, called by his reincarnation name Tenzin Gyatso (Jetsun Jamphel Ngawang Lobsang Yeshe Tenzin Gyatso) was revealed in 1939. It was after the death of the 13th Dalai Lama (called by his reincarnation name Thupten Gyatso) that the monks in charge of finding the next Dalai Lama set out in search of him in a faraway land. Before the members of the mission who then presented themselves to him as mere pilgrims, the two-year-old boy, Lhamo Dhondup, recognized objects belonging to the 13th Dalai Lama and spoke the dialect of his previous incarnation:

« When the research team joined us... They said I had spoken the Lhasa dialect. I don't remember, but my mother confirmed that I had spoken with the members of the research team in a language she did not understand. This means that I used the language of my previous life. [48] »

Reincarnation is admitted by Tibetans in theory and practice as a spiritual entity connected to the material body, but not entirely dependent on it, which separates itself from it at death. This entity then migrates, and is led to a new body, as one leaves one worn garment to put on another, which is imposed by the automatic interplay of causes and effects. The causes that determine the nature of reincarnation are acts performed in several past existences. Thus the activities of

the body, speech and spirit manufacture the destiny of the individual in his continued existence, from reincarnation to
reincarnation, through the succession of deaths and births.

• 51.4 – Judaism

In Judaism, between the 6th century B.C. until the 1st century
and during the so-called *Second Temple* period, there is no
obvious trace of reincarnation; the idea only appears in the
eighth century in the mystical and esoteric tradition of the
Kabbalah.

The concept used in Hebrew is that of «Guilgoul hanesha-
mot» more simply called «guilgoul» or «gilgul», in Hebrew
גלגול הנשמות, litt. | cycle of souls | a term that refers to the
cyclic crossing of lives, or incarnations attached to different
physical bodies over time. The body they associate with depends on their particular task in the physical world, the level
of spirituality or previous incarnations.

• 51.5 – Christianity

In Christianity, metempsychosis was condemned in 553, at
the Ecumenical Council of Constantinople, to defend the ori-

ginality of resurrection.

Nevertheless, the incarnation, *God who becomes flesh*, or the *resurrection*, could also refer to *metensomatosis*: once the soul has left the body, it sojourns in Purgatory, Paradise or Hell, waiting for the Last Day and the return of Christ who will judge the living and the dead and raise them up.

• 51.6 – Islam

In Islam, the idea of reincarnation is officially rejected. But the idea is retained and promulgated by the Imams of some traditions. It would be more accurate to say that readers of sacred texts must use their free will to decide. Imam Abdullah in *A Muslim Vision of the Soul* promotes this idea by highlighting the sacred texts:

> « We Muslims believe in the existence of the soul, and say that man is composed of a body and a soul. [1,1] – when a man dies, his soul leaves his body. [1,2] the soul is then led by angels...[1,3] who lead and lift it up into the heavens [1,4] »

• 51.7 – Greek Antiquity

In the 6th century BC, it is mainly thanks to Greek thinkers, possibly inspired by Hinduism that the principles of reincarnation and metempsychosis flourished, those of the « transmigration of souls » *or of a « renaissance in succession ».* The *soul* continues its evolution from human existence into existence and can possibly be embodied in an animal or a plant.

In the 6th c. BC, Pythagoras, reformer, mathematician, philosopher and first adept of vegetarianism, thought that the soul is immortal and that it passes, in other animal species; he says he can remember not only his own previous lives or the bodies his soul has occupied, but also the past lives of those he encounters:

> « According to Heraclides of Pontus, this is what he himself recounted on his account: he had once been Ethaliad, who was called the son of Mercury; that god had promised to grant him all that he wanted, except immortality, he had asked to keep the memory of all that would befall him in his life and after his death; and indeed, alive and dead,

he had kept the memory of all things...

[he] declared that he had previously been Ethaliad that Mercury had given him the consciousness of the migrations of his soul, and that he remembered in which plants, in which animals she had successively passed...

he then remembered that he was first Ethaliad, then Euphorbus, then Hermotime and finally Pyrrhus. After the death of Pyrrhus, he had become Pythagoras and had kept the same memories. [85] »

PLATON PYTHAGORE

Fig. 19

In his theory of transmigration of souls, Pythagoras admits a type of reincarnation comparable to that in Hinduism or Jainism, because his belief in metempsychosis corresponds to a soul that can come and slide in a non-human, vegetable or animal body:

« He spent a day with a young dog being abused; He

took pity, they say, and cried out:

Stop, stop knocking; This is my friend,

it is his soul; I recognized him by his voice. [85] »

Pythagoras died in 495 and Plato was born some seventy years later, in 428 BC.

He, in turn, asserts that 1,000 years elapse between death and rebirth, and he supports the idea of reincarnation in many of his works. In *Phaedon*, he stages the last moments of Socrates's life and presents a dual separation between body and soul that survives death; by separating from the body, the *soul* finds, an intelligible world left only temporarily:

« Our soul is very similar to that which is divine, immortal, intelligible, simple, indissoluble, always the same, and always similar to itself, and...our body resembles... to that which is human, mortal, sensitive, composed, dissoluble, ever-changing, and never like itself;

...at death, the soul is led where the dead are gathered to be judged, and then taken to the Other World where, at the end of a given time... they are brought back to life after long and numerous revolutions of centuries;

The soul... in this state goes to what is similar to it... and there it is happy, free from mistakes, from madness, from fears, from disordered love and from all the other evils of humans; and as the initiates say, the *soul* truly spends eternity with the gods... [65]»

ART. 52 – The West and Reincarnation

At the beginning of the 19th century, reincarnation was popularized in the West by various spiritual, spiritist or esoteric currents, in many fields of philosophy, metaphysics, psychology, and psychiatry.

• 52.1 – 1857 • Allan Kardec

In 1857, Denizard Hippolyte-Léon Rivail, *alias* Allan Kardec — a name his name from a previous incarnation when he was a Druid — published *The Book of Spirits*, the founding work of spiritualism which he said he was the channeler, and which specified:

> « The spiritual doctrine naturally rests on the existence within us of a being independent of matter and survivor of the body... There are three things in man: 1° the body or material being analogous to animals, and animated by the same vital principle; 2° the soul or immaterial being, the Spirit incarnate in the body; 3° the bond that unites the soul and the body, the intermediate principle between matter and the Spirit...

Man thus has two natures: by his body, he participates in the nature of animals of which he has the instincts; through his soul he partakes of the nature of Spirits. [42] »

• 52.2 – 1880 • Friedrich Nietzsche

For Friedrich Nietzsche, a German philosopher, cultural critic, composer, poet, writer and philologist whose work has had a profound influence on contemporary intellectual history, life is an incessant dance loop that breaks and re-forms, as he testifies in the third part of *Thus Spoke Zarathustra, The Convalescent*:

« O Zarathustra,... it is the things themselves that dance: all comes and stretches out their hand, and laughs, and flees — and returns." All is broken, all is assembled again; Eternally the same house of being builds. Everything separates, all greets again; the ring of existence remains eternally faithful to itself. [59] »

• 52.3 – 1910 • Jiddu Krishnamurti

Philosopher and free thinker, Jiddu Krishnamurti, puts forward the idea that a *radical metamorphosis* of humanity comes first, by overcoming the fear of death that can only be accomplished by freeing oneself from known or preconceived ideas:

> « We believe that living always takes place in the present and that dying is an event that awaits us in the distant future... We want evidence of the survival of the *soul,* we listen to the statements of psychics, and the results of psychical research... In general, we are afraid to die because we do not know what it means to live. [45]"

> ...

> « What [humanity] needs is something totally new...a mutation of the psyche itself. [45] »

• 52.4 – 1960 • The Hippie Movement

The hippie counter-culture movement of the 1960s that preached, 'Let's make love, not war!' under the slogan *peace and love* took over the expansion of the concept of reincarnation and its popularization in the West.

The beatniks distinguished themselves by their conscious and deliberate opposition to the dominant culture in all the countries where they settled. They no longer shared the collective ideals of previous generations; they rejected the establishment, liberalism, communism, anti-fascism, and all ...*isms,* social conventions or the regular work work work state of mind; they distanced themselves from family structures, conventional education, dogmatism and had no taboo regarding nudity or sexuality, especially with regard to homosexuality.

Their movement conveyed new values: the music by Jimi Hendrix, Bob Marley, Joan Baez, Janis Joplin, Joe Cocker, The Who, the Plastic Ono Band, along with peace activists John Lennon and Yoko Ono, the famous *Let It Be* or *Imagine*, Rasta philosophy, bellbottoms, ethnic dresses, loose-fitting ties and dye or dreadlocks, and men are no longer ashamed to cry, wear pink or flower shirts.

The hippies went en masse, to Asia especially to India or Tibet, to meet the greatest gurus of the time and to soak up new spiritual values: those of Hinduism and Mahāyāna, Theravāda or Zen Buddhism.

The journey and the breathtaking discovery of the vast wild spaces of Tibet or Mongolia, the eastern religions, the artificial paradises linked to psychedelic drugs are part of their daily life, but also kindness, the fusion with nature, trekking to the highest peaks, natural and gentle medicines, or the letting go of the ego. They are interested in other cultures and sharing, respect and empathy become essential values.

The Gurus, Sensei, Rōshis, Lamas, Guides and Spiritual Masters of Asia, faced with this tide of curious new spirits from the Eastern heavens, took advantage of it to develop Meditation centers and adapted techniques: Jiddu Krishnamurti, the author of *Freedom From The Known*, created Educational Centres under the label of the Krishnamurti Foundation Trust in Brockwood Park and Oak Grove, USA and India; Maharishi Mahesh Yogi developed *Transcendental Meditation*; Swami Prabhupada, *The Hare Krishna and the International Associa-*

tion for Krishna Consciousness.

Very vast city-size ashrams were built under the influence of renowned Gurus, in particular, the French Mirra Alfassa Richard, *alias* La Mère, Sri Aurobindo's spiritual companion, who in 1968, created *Auroville*, a laboratory city shaped like a spiral galaxy, designed to accommodate 50,000 inhabitants, near Pondicherry, the former French East India Company.

Large developments were also undertaken by the very controversial Bhagwan Shree Rajneesh *alias* Osho, in Rajneeshpuram *(Oregon, USA),* and by Sathya Sai Baba: two free hospitals, an educational complex that includes schools, free colleges and universities approved by the Indian government and a project for the supply of drinking water to the 5 million inhabitants of the city of Chennai (ex-Madras).

The list of gurus is long and has influenced the West: Nisargadatta Marahaj, Vivekananda, Muktananda, Ma Ananda Moyi, Vimala Tarkar, Mahasi Sayadaw or S.H. Goenka... The hippies and all the meditation and personal development centers of the West or the East were the first to have integrated, adapted and then widely disseminated the concept of reincarnation.

ART. 53 – Academic Science and Reincarnation

Convince the scientific community of the validity of a reality that escapes the majority of conventional scientists was the goal of those who were interested in the cases of people who remember living on other planets and actually being on a mission on Earth, that is to say « stellar reincarnations ». They are also called Star-Seeds or Wanderers. Science generally gives no credit to the explanation of these extraterrestrial stories, and the absence of tangible material proof makes them prefer medicine, psychiatry and sociology.

• 53.1 – 1960 • Ian Stevenson

In the West, one of the best-known scientists and academics who worked on the issue of reincarnation was Canadian psychiatrist Ian Stevenson. He was the Director of the Division of Personality Studies and a Professor in the Department of Psychiatry at the University of Virginia, Charlottesville, USA.

He is known to have tried to scientifically analyze reincarnation cases and he spent 40 years, from 1967 until his death in 2007, collecting 1,400 cases of children who remembered their past lives and published them under the title *Children Who Remember Their Past Lives* – Here is the text on the back cover of the book:

« Ian Stevenson discusses some of the frequently asked questions about children claiming to remember past lives. - Why are we more likely to remember certain lives, especially those that have had a violent end? - Why do almost all children, between the ages of five and seven, forget the earliest memories of their previous lives? - Why are there more cases in Asia and parts of Africa than in the West? - What are the main interpretations of these cases, apart from reincarnation? - Why, in some cases, does reincarnation seem to be the best interpretation? Ian Stevenson describes, for the general public, his twenty-five-year research on cases of children who say they remember a previous life. He explains, in clear and accessible language, how he conducted his research, the important results he obtained and the conclusions he drew from them. [73] »

His research was criticized and Jim B. Tucker, of the Department of Perceptual Studies at the same university, in an essay published in 2008, in the *Journal of Scientific Exploration*, reports that Stevenson wrote:

« [he] had collected data that allowed those who found reincarnation an acceptable concept to believe in, on the basis of a collection of evidence, rather than on the basis of belief alone (Stevenson, 1980, 1990b). This group of people, however, was not the one he most wanted to convince. One day he said – with a smile – that his death would be a fiasco because he had failed to achieve his main objective, which was to get the scientific community to consider reincarnation, a valid and serious research hypothesis. [77] »

• 53.2 – 1970 • The Invisible College

From 1960 to 1975 — with Jacques Vallée, a French mathematician, astrophysicist, computer scientist, ufologist and author residing in the USA, and the pioneer of French ufology, Aimé Michel, writer as well as the American Joseph Allen Hynek, the French Pierre Guérin, Claude Poher and Yves Rocard — the Invisible College will provide a discreet network for information exchange and research. They are convinced that there is a coordinated and intentional intelligence behind UFO manifestations and that it would be possible to prove

that the Earth is subject to widespread and systematic surveillance and control. The issue is obviously of importance,
since it is a matter of undertaking serious scientific studies
and obtaining valid results to solve the UFO enigma.

> « The work of the « Invisible College» is revolutionary
> because the scientists who are members (a hundred
> in five or six countries) challenge a certain conception
> of scientific authority when they affirm that these
> strange observations deserve to be studied, and that
> no theory about them, no matter how fantastic,
> should be rejected without analysis. [82] »

Vallée sees in the ufological phenomenon, a sociological
event structuring society, a system of evolutionary control
exerted on the collective unconscious, through phenomena
or parapsychological stratagems. The author's perspective is
expressed in his trilogy or in his UFO works: *the great manipulation* or *Revelations: contact with another world or human manipulation?*

Vallée will witness a UFO overflight and will closely follow the
wave of 1954 which sees a surge of spacecrafts flying over Europe; his passion for occultism, especially for the Rosicru-

cians, will feed his discourses on reincarnation:

The very term Rose-Cross refers to the one who has reached the Christian state of spiritual and moral perfection, the Rosicrucians trying to attain this degree of enlightenment, the profound nature of the Rose-Cross being situated, like spiritual Alchemy, in the individual inner experience. Although the Order of the Rose-Cross did not appear until the seventeenth century, tradition made Paracelsus (1493-1541), an emblematic physician and alchemist, one of the first Rosicrucians. These correspondences with alchemy are also found in the beliefs attached to them. Thus, the Rosicrucians distinguish the human soul and the athanor, that is, the physical body and the subtle bodies that keep the latter alive and ensure the bond with the soul, which proceeds from God. Human existence is then thought of as the ground of this elevation of man, a transmutation, which also reveals to him his close ties with God and Nature. The Rosicrucian teachings therefore question the true nature of the Divine, the origin of the universe, the structure of matter, the concepts of time and space, the laws of life, the purpose of evolution, the human soul and its attributes, the phases of consciousness, psychic phenomena, the mysteries of death, afterlife and reincarnation, traditional symbolism and also nurture many ancient techniques in mysticism such as relaxation, concentration, meditation, mental creation, spiritual alchemy, etc. [82] »

In 1966, Aimé Michel published an article entitled *Le problème de la réincarnation* where he addressed the scientific study in this field:

« In physics, chemistry, biology, we respect the researcher. But before we admit a discovery, we control it. This is not suspicion. It is a method. To believe without control and reject without examination bears witness to an identical failure of thought. The facts put forward by Indian and American researchers seem convincing. They join other facts studied at the beginning of this century by Colonel de Rochas in France and by *the Society for Psychical Research* in London. Their indisputable similarity strongly suggests that there is something real here. And that something would be of such a consequence and would so profoundly alter our deepest assessments—meaning of life and death, man's situation in the universe, a sense of effort, suffering and love — which science can legitimately be expected to apply its methods to, if possible. And do we know exactly what is possible and what is not? How would we know if we didn't try? Until now, the fear of Western thought in the face of death has led it either to act as if the problem did not exist, even to exorcise it by sarcasm, or to seek absolute solutions by metaphysical religious ways. Without discussing the validity of these solutions, it must be noted that they are incommunicable. What if death was a stupid problem *as well*, justiciable with the stupid small methods — observation, experimentation, measurement — that enabled man to control his physical environment, to defeat tuberculosis, to release atomic energy and to go to the Moon? Have we so far found better than these little methods? [56] »

• 53.3 – 1980 • John E. Mack

In terms of scientific impregnation, and although John Edward Mack's work central theme was not reincarnation per se, but alien abductions, resistance and tacit or agreed academic protocols, can be a challenge that very few researchers dare to take up when the motto is "stay on track".

But Mack, embarked on this path. At the time, he was an American psychiatrist, writer and professor at Harvard Medical School, Cambridge, USA, where he founded the psychiatric teaching unit; he became an authority in hypnosis by studying the effects on the human psyche of cases of alien abductions. His interest in the transformational aspects of extraordinary experiences corresponded to his own conviction that the Western world had to move away from an eminently materialistic view of the world;

> « The abductions are similar to a psychological and spiritual experience that occurs and perhaps originates in another dimension. So these are phenomena that open us, or at least force us to be open to realities that do not belong solely to our physical world. [52] »

He published some of the clinical results of his research in his book *Extraterrestrial Files – The Case of Abduction - Human Encounters with Aliens*:

> « In spite of my deep admiration and respect for pioneers in this field such as Budd Hopkins, who had the courage to investigate, to study, to analyze and communicate the results of their work against all our culture and systems of thought, I had to present in this book my own clinical investigations. The subject before us is the subject of so much controversy that no recognized scientific authority has ventured to analyze or develop what could be used today to support my arguments or conclusions. Therefore, I can only explain what I have learned little by little, on the job, with each of the cases that have arisen, and formulate alone my interpretations as my conclusions on the basis of this same information. [52] »

This book came as a shock and its publication in the United States, in 1994, provoked an unprecedented controversy. Believing that Mack had failed to meet the standards and direction of academic research, the dean asked an ethics commit-tee to assess the validity of his work. He was not suspected of any ethical violation or improper conduct and had not viola-ted the ethical rules of the profession. The complaint was wi-thdrawn two years later, but Mack was nonetheless censored for methodological errors. [52]

• 53.4 – 2020 • Jean-Pierre Petit

Research director at the CNRS (the French National Centre for Scientific Research), astrophysicist, author of more than one hundred publications in the fields of cosmology and plasma physics, with Jean-Claude Bourret, editor-in-chief, at FR3, France Inter, TF1, co-wrote *Metaphysicon. We Have A Soul That Survives After Death. This Is Scientifically Proven*, in which physics and metaphysics merge.

According to the authors, we do have a *soul* that would mi-grate after death through a tunnel that connects two worlds: the physical world and the metaphysical world as shown in the illustration below, taken from their work [64]. This tunnel would be the same one described by people who had a NDE (Near Death Experience).

Petit explains:

« Let us agree that all the positive masses correspond to what will be called reality. This other
matter, which I will call a metamatter, corresponds to another plane, to another form of reality. I will immediately refer to two qualifiers.

The masses which we consider to correspond to
what we call reality, obey the laws of physics. But
these other masses will obey the laws of metaphysics... In this metaphysical world, we will have
meta-particles, carrying electrical meta-charges,
undergoing meta-forces. These particles will interact with each other through meta-radiation.

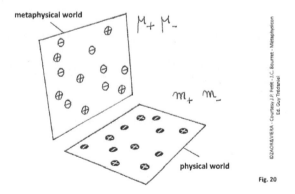

Fig. 20

In principle, a scientific mission is to examine the reality of phenomena. Phenomena such as feelings or thoughts are certainly difficult to put between slides and coverslips. But there remains an experience that all human beings experience one day or another, it is death...

An observable that no physicist can deny. Physics gives only a phenomenological description of death. Bodily functions slow down gradually. The heart stops, the brain waves change until they shut down. We are all brought to experience such an event... Everything happens as if a human being is a kind of box with something inside that is called consciousness. That's what conventional science says when you talk to it. When death intervenes, that something disappears. There is no longer a correspondent online. According to science, at the time of death this something, indefinable, would be annihilated, destroyed. According to different religious beliefs, this something would survive even after the 'box' was destroyed. But here, religions provide us with an answer in the form of a belief, a faith. And from this angle, science has its own answer, equally devoid of justification.

In fact, science does not even explicitly express this idea. By concentrating on life, science turns her back on death, as we would with a taboo. Those who pretend to medically study NDEs, *Near-Death Experience,* flirt with the practice ban, issued by the General Medical Council. Compared to the alleged phenomena, the medical doxa opposes all kinds of interpretations.

The light tunnel described by subjects who have experienced these states would then be related to the functioning of the retina, whose dysfunction before death would narrow the visual field. As for the sensations reported, they are then attributed to the action of endorphins that would be secreted by the body. [64] »

• 53.5 – 2021 • T.I.M. Zaor & Viera

A similar hypothesis of — two merged worlds, not dependent on the continuum of space-time, where everything is and is not at the same time, a physical reality and an alternative reality — is clearly posed by T.I.M. Zaor & Viera in *1793, Marie-Antoinette – Cosmic transmutation* when Marie-Antoinette realizes that, even if Samson gave her death, she passes into a reality yet unknown to her, where her consciousness is still alive:

A roll of drums sounds, then I hear the dry sound of a click.

The executioner concentrates, opens his fingers, as if to regret and releases the rope.

Fear expels ten thousand joules of energy into my body at once, a torrent of adrenaline rushes into my veins, and as if it could, my whole being tries to escape from its prison of flesh; I'm on the verge of fainting, I'm suffocating, I feel like my heart is going to explode; I try to remove my head stuck in the hole of the guillotine or to release my wrists, in vain; all my muscles contract in an attempt to protect me from the impact;

the slicer comes down with a single stream, with the crunch of iron, the slow and gentle whispering of a blade passing over a stone, the rubbing of the knife along the grooves on the posts, like the rustling of skis sliding on fresh snow, a bright and sunny winter day. It lasts, it lasts and it never ends. I wish I could have suspended this moment and never experienced it.

Sharpened on one side, the blade slides by the bezel and acts like huge scissors. I feel its deadly breath on my skin; its spike cuts into my dermis, slices my flesh, severs my vertebrae, cuts my throat, and eventually through my vocal cords; then it stops abruptly, steel against wood; my head thus released, falls on the sawdust in the basket below me, with the dull sound of a biological waste that has just been thrown on a pile of compost.

Expelled from my head, the thick and warm blood begins to gush out accompanied by bitter mixed odors of sap and iron. My consciousness begins to dissipate; Life escapes from my body. I tried to blink my eyelids in a desperate effort to keep them open and saw the top edge of the basket and clouds.

I exist! I said to myself, not believing it, *I exist!*
The public Executioner grabs me my hair and holds my head high, screaming.

— Long live the Republic!

... My head swayed under the executioner's movements and oscillated from right to left, to the rhythm of his steps on the platform; I clearly saw the place rocking, the sky swirling, the buildings and houses wobbling, and the soldiers and the guns unmoved. In a final effort, I tried to say they should not feel guilty that this choice to accept the cleaver, I had made with them, so that this world, which I had helped shape, and which they had ended up hating, would come to an end.

What I wanted to tell them is that death is not the end, it's the beginning. They understood everything backwards.

...

When the body stopped physically and clinical death occurred, it was about five minutes before

294

serious brain damage occurred, and despite the fact that my head was separated from my body, my consciousness did not stop immediately. In response to the first moments of the agony, my lungs had synthesized dimethyltryptamine *(DMT)* produced naturally in very small amounts by the pineal gland, the epiphysis.

The brain doesn't have a lot of time and it takes it out of the blood, passes it through the neural membranes and concentrates it in the nerve cells to keep the brain alive longer. A succession of stops and revivals of consciousness followed, in rhythm, each contraction and the outbursts of blood.

My visual acuity increased. Forms that seemed to be underwater, with bright colors enveloped my environment and were accompanied by soft, prolonged tinnitus, with dull and deep notes.

I thought there was nothing after death, that it was a big black hole and gaping. But I was wrong. On the contrary, I noticed that I was suspended between two states, like a child being born: more completely fetus and not yet newborn, an *anima*, the Life, the breath, of the Greek verb *psuchein*, in Hebrew *Nèphèsh,* breathe, *the vital principle* of Aristotle.

Strangely enough, I still felt like I was still alive when I no longer belonged to the physical world and I could see, hear, feel and touch, all senses amalgamated.

Reality was fluid space, pulsed in slow motion, as if it were alive, full of light and diffuse sounds; it seemed to molt, extend and collapse all at once, in a dimension out of time that had, moreover, suddenly stopped. Everything seemed latent and manifest.

The autonomy of my consciousness lasted long enough to feel life leave: my brain ended up beating empty, in systole, then came the cerebral arrest, the cognitive arrest, the energetic arrest, the fragmented arrest of my consciousness. My lips waved in a silent stammering.

To my surprise, I realized that I was walking in space, outside my body. I was floating, way above the guillotine; I watched the scene, the executioner and his helpers; I could see my head in the basket, my body disappearing through a hatch on the floor, the buckets of water thrown away for cleaning.

The place was emptying; the drums, the soldiers and the crowd were leaving.

I felt my energy slowly slide from matter to something impalpable, as one passes from water to air, coming out of a bath.

It was a very curious feeling, something new that I had never felt before. I was now evolving into an alternative reality, and I felt at home, immersed in a warm amber liquid that I was breathing, like a fetus in the womb of a mother, surrounded by a background of a Klein blue, transcendental and cosmic light. [84]

ART. 54 – Women and reincarnation

• 54.1 – 1910 • Alexandra David-Néel

French explorer, anthropologist, writer and tibetologist Alexandra David-Néel, was in 1924 the first Western woman to enter Lhasa, the capital of Tibet, disguised as a beggar, a feat that contributed to her international fame. In 1961, she published a book entirely dedicated to *Immortality and Reincarnation. Doctrines and practices. China – Tibet - India,* a section on Tibetan ritualistic practices of transference to a body:

> Associated with the reading of the Bardo thös tol or, more briefly practiced alone, a rite called *powa* is also, held as proper to perform the transference... All Tibetans believe that death is the beginning of an arduous journey, full of perils, that man must make in the interval that will elapse until a new reincarnation in one or the other of the six categories of beings to which the journey will end.
>
> The regions the deceased will have to cross are

described according to the landscapes familiar to Tibetans. The *soul* will have to climb high mountains along steep paths, ford wide and fast rivers, deserted and arid regions and everywhere demons are on the alert, as well as brigands. Tibetans are practical people and have the charitable thought of strengthening the dying or the deceased, in view of the journey he will undertake. For this purpose a meal will be served several times a day as long as the body remains at home waiting for the day of the funeral.

The period between the time of death and the day of the funeral is always long. Cutting it off would appear to be a lack of respect or an anxious feeling to quickly get rid of the deceased. It is also appropriate, in a country where the villages are as far apart as they are in Tibet, to give the guests enough time to make a journey of two to three hundred kilometers, or more, and arduous paths, through the mountains...

The bodies of eminent personalities, especially those of the Great Lamas, are embalmed or mummified and enveloped in salt. The body of the last Penechin Lama, who died in Chinese territory when he was going back to Tibet, was preserved in this way. Every day, the wet salt was replaced by fresh salt... Another method of preserving the body of a Grand Lama is to immerse it in a bath of boiling butter. Then, the mummy's figure is spread with gold, the mummy is dressed, and can remain exposed in a glass case. These mummies are called: *mardong, butter figures.*

As for the vast majority of the deceased, they are dressed in their finest clothes. Instead of being normally fastened, the front of the garment is placed on the dead man's back. This, it seems, is a way of making the deceased understand that they no longer belong to the world of the living, as they may not have realized it yet. [23] »

• 54.2 – 1960 • Mirra Alfassa *aka* La Mère

Mirra Alfassa Richard of France, *aka* La Mère, Sri Aurobindo 's spiritual companion, who created *Auroville* in 1968, wrote:

> « The earth needs a place where people can live free from all national rivalries, all social conventions, all contradictory morality and all antagonistic religions; a place where, freed from all the slavery of the past, human beings can devote themselves totally to the discovery and the practical application of the Divine Consciousness that wants to manifest. *Auroville* wants to be this place to all those who aspire to live the truth of tomorrow. [2] »

while conveying Sri Aurobindo's view on incarnation:

> « Even if science — be it physical or occult — discovered the conditions or means necessary for the body to survive indefinitely, and the body nevertheless could not adapt to become an adequate instrument for expressing inner growth, the soul would then find a way to abandon it and reincarnate.

The material, physical causes of death are not its only or true cause; his deepest reason is a spiritual necessity for the evolution of a new being. [5] »

In the West, many ideas related to Eastern religions are now normalized and the concept of reincarnation is more freely evoked in academic debates on immortality.

The phenomenon goes far beyond mere interest or influence. Today it is of a different magnitude, says Dr. Janet Cunningham, President of the International Board for *Regression Therapy,* an organization that brings together therapists who specialize in reincarnation research:

> « We are not talking about a small minority that is passionate about something for a few months, but about a change of collective mindset, people are increasingly open to other universes. They also face religious institutions that are very rigid and no longer meet their aspirations. It is observed that many people change denominations or study other religions and their practices. [20] »

• 54.3 – 2000 • Dolores Cannon

Dolores Cannon, born in 1931 in Missouri, United States, is a pioneer in the field of regression through hypnosis and the recovery of past lives memory. After her first exposure to the concept of reincarnation in 1968, she specialized in regression therapy and the collection and cataloguing of lost knowledge.

She created an academy offering the learning of a unique technique of deep hypnosis, the *Quantum Healing Hypnosis Therapy* (QHHT) and published eighteen books on her research concerning hypnosis and cases of contact or abduction by extraterrestrials.

For fifteen years of in-depth research, Cannon asserts that by going back to one's birth and going beyond, this technique makes it possible to discover the laws of the Universe, the lessons to be learned before the next rebirth and to plan the next incarnation. In *Between Life and Death*, Cannon states that, during dreams, everyone can go to 'intermediate universes' located between life and death, to carry out or execute programmed missions. [12]

In *The Three Waves of Volunteers*, she introduces the notion of waves of people of stellar origin who, for about fifty years, consciously program to be reborn on Earth to help improve human conditions: the waves of the Indigo, Cristal and Rainbow children. She offers an explanation of the relatively recent phenomenon of these new souls incarnated on Earth, spiritually advanced and having great difficulty finding their marks. [12]

In the US, one in four people now believe in reincarnation. In 2009, Bruce and Andrea Leininger and Ken Gross published *The Soul Survivor,* based on a child's experience as a pilot during the Second World War; their book was a great success in bookstores and seminars on this topic now bring together thousands of people.

- **54.4 – 2020 • Carol Bowman**

The first two books by Carol Bowman, a therapist and speaker known for her work on the study of reincarnation cases involving young children *Children's Past Lives* and *Return From Heaven,* have become classics and have been translated into twenty-three languages.

In Pennsylvania, Carol Bowman uses relaxation techniques to engage with her patients. She says she can give many examples of cases where the only possible explanation for understanding her clients' visions is the possibility of having lived another life.

The Internet has certainly contributed greatly to making the various theories on reincarnation more accessible. Discussion forums on past lives are legion and generate thousands of comments. On Carol Bowman's website, and her *Reincarnation Forum*, a young woman, identified as Jennywren, tells how her daughter Lottie began to evoke memories that would date back to the year 1787, at the age of 2:

> « It all started when she was 2 years old. We were walking around when she surprised me by telling me she remembered *1787*. I wondered how she knew it was a year and how, at two years old, she knew how to say it.
>
> A few weeks later...she pointed out that her first name was *Daisy* and her last name was *Robinson,* that she was once Daisy Robinson. (She did not

know anyone by that name)... she was married...and weaving blankets... in the following weeks, she told us that she had also been a boy, that she lived in Germany, spoke German and married in France... I think the thing that touched me the most was that one day, Lottie came up to me in the kitchen and said,

— *all the air came out of here.*

I didn't know what she was talking about so I asked:

"*Where did it come from?*"

Lottie pointed the middle of her body with her finger and said:

— *Here. And I am dead.*

But I don't like to talk about it.

It really shook me, because I had no idea that my two-year-old daughter knew what death was or that people could die!

She went on to say that she was 30 when she died and that it was because she was hungry.

[Note from the author: There was indeed a famine in 1787 – There was terrible dry spring and hot summer, followed by floods and very severe winters which reduced the harvests and a great famine settled for several years in France and some other countries in Europe.]

But it was the case for John E. Mack, there have been many criticisms from the scientific community. With the public growing interest, the methods used by *regressive hypnotists* especially when applied to children, are highly questioned by conventional psychiatrists.

« The problem is that it is impossible to verify what happens during these sessions, » says Dr. Jim Tucker, a psychiatrist at the University of Virginia, who studies cases of children claiming to have had previous lives.

Thus, the *International Board for Regression Therapy*, was set up in 1997 with the help of Janet Cunningham, to formalize certain practices and issue licenses to therapists who apply a rigorous and recognized protocol.

ART. 55 – Stellar (extraterrestrial) and reincarnation

Do stars recognize the existence of a soul? Is there a tangible reality after death? Do stellars (aliens) die? Is death the same as on Earth? Do they reincarnate?

We had to walk historically and chronologically from prehistoric to modern Earth times, to grasp the multiple concepts of the *soul* from the stellar (extraterrestrial) point of view, because they are inclusive of Earth concepts.

As with the terrestrial concept, it is preferable not to generalize as it is impossible to give a uniform definition. There is not a single concept of the soul for all stellar lineages, but a multitude that depends on their belief systems, their planets, their societies, their cultures or their religions and that are as diverse as those of Earthlings.

As on Earth, the same planet may have different beliefs depending on the territories, lineages or peoples that occupy them and their scientific, theological or philosophical systems, can sometimes be similar to Earth systems or very different. There is no single way to define the concept of an extraterrestrial *soul*.

- **55.1 – The Extraterrestrial *Soul***

Some stellar (extraterrestrial) races observe the evolution of individuals as *souls*, from what could be called 'the birth of a soul' throughout successive incarnations, development and spiritual maturation; thus they determine whether a person or peoples are physically, morally, intellectually or spiritually ready to interact with them as equals.

Life, for the vast majority of stellars (extraterrestrials) is neither linear, nor chronological, nor limited to a particular physical form. They regard the body as precious and speak of many *souls* who are awaiting integration into a body. They think that it is a piece of clothing made of flesh and bone, a biological envelope that a person occupies the time of his temporary time on a planet, in a given community.

The person goes from body to body, from incarnation to incarnation, on this planet and then others, with the aim of achieving spiritual integration, self-realization in mineral, animal or plant bodies. They therefore apprehend humans, animals, plants and rocks at the same level. They themselves remember their last incarnations, as if it were the childhood of their present life.

They stress that the cycles of birth and rebirth allow us to choose to ascend, and that the death of the body is not necessary to do so. Realizing oneself and breaking the veil of oblivion can be done during one's lifetime. Realization is unconditional and therefore does not depend on any materiality or space-time.

They do not regard the experience of leaving the body as a death, for it is not the cessation of existence or consciousness. It is only a tool that has come to an end, a temporary incarnation, one step among many. It is a natural part of reincarnation for a time-limited sensory learning experience limited to 3D. The soul then reincarnates into another body-garment for the continuation of a temporal experience.

Let's look at a few examples of extraterrestrial belief in reincarnation:

• 55.2 — Stellar Lineage A
Human-type bipeds (categorized as such).

They are organized in a patriarchal society (a social system dominated by male authority), scientific, eminently logical, a strict societal organization and a dictatorial governance with four heads, aided by a planetary artificial intelligence; they have a religious system very similar to Christianity with a faith in a central figure, considered a Messiah, similar to Jesus

Christ. He too lived a life of suffering, imprisonment and torture and sacrificed himself to save the lives of the people who were then under the despotic and tyrannical yoke of a leader. His body was dematerialized at the time of death, under the eyes of witnesses. This lineage of stellars (extraterrestrials) believes in God and their concept of the *soul* is similar to that of Christianity presented in Art. 42.

• 55.3 — Stellar Lineage B
Human Bipeds (other, not categorized as such).

They are organized in a balanced patriarchal-matriarchal society (50%-men and 50%-women), scientific, logical and reasoned, a samsaric societal organization, a philosophical system identical to Buddhism, a belief centered on karma, and for good reason: they are the ones who seeded it on Earth in Ancient Times. They therefore follow the great principles of *karma* and all their life and actions are centered on events, causes and effects and emptiness. They have no god, but Wise Elders. Their concept of *soul* is identical to that presented in Art. 40.

• 55.4 — Stellar Lineage C
Human-type bipeds (categorized as such).

They are organized in a matriarchal royalty (social system dominated by feminine authority, in this case, domineering), scientific, with an eminently developed affect, a holographic societal organization – from the ancient Greek ὅλος, *hólos* meaning *'whole'* (without duality) – organized in Level Councils, from Family Council to Planetary Council and a composite belief system:

- animism, a belief in which all living beings, including objects, can dispose of a soul,

- paganism, individuals are connected to each other, and the latter to a cosmos where the divine is everywhere, and not separated from a "profane" world,

- Greek polytheism, women especially gather in Greek *Olympian Pantheon* type Councils with mythological Greek Goddess names and powers,

- and some principles of quantum mechanics.

Their belief is centered on the notion of *Original Source*, fractalized into multiple *souls,* which would be fragments of it. Their concept of the *soul* is a composite of those presented in Art. 38 (prehistory), 44 (Greek antiquity), and 49 (physics).

• 55.5 — Stellar Lineage D
Exomorph bipeds that can easily use their four limbs

they have a head, a trunk and limbs, but are plant-like and asexual exomorphs.

They are organized into functional swarms or apiaries, without central governance, without female or male genders, without reproductive system, and without affect; it is a societal statistician system from which their belief system based on statistics derives. Their calculations of Earth's *soul* population add up to only 10%. Rather, their concept of the soul is the deeply rooted sense of their community which could be called an egregore. Egregore is an immaterial structure, designating a group spirit consisting of the aggregation of the strategies, intentions, energies and actions of the individuals who make up the group. On Earth, this term refers to group dynamics or team spirit. The human race, for them, is only the result of a set of random emergence, not specific to beings with complex structures.

• **55.6 - Commonalities**

All stellar (extraterrestrial) lineages perceive the *soul* in the same way they see an *aura.* It is:

• **a signal, with a frequency spectrum** •

A *soul* is a signal, a set with a frequency spectrum that can be measured using a technology similar to the frequency meter or mass spectrometer, and analyzed graphically on a screen. Stellars (extraterrestrials) measure an *aura* which is electromagnetic radiation projected by a body, and they can determine the stellar lineage and all the incarnations of a person, whether earthly or extraterrestrial,

• **immortal** •

The *soul* never dies, it transforms or moves. If the physical body of the stellar lineages (extraterrestrials) can have a much greater longevity than that of the Earthlings, there are some for which, the *soul* and the physical body that self-regulates and molts, are immortal.
On the other hand, whether the body dies or not, the *soul*

that is related or associated with this body is an *autonomous supra-system* independent of bodily physicality. This *supra-system* can migrate from one living body to another, or transmigrate to a new body, upon death. It can also be artificially transmuted from one body to another thanks to their technologies.

ART. 56 – Stellar Emissaries (StarSeeds) and Terrestrial Natives (EarthSeeds): Bodies and *Souls*
What are the differences between StarSeeds and EarthSeeds?

In a conventional way, people who have a *soul*, come from another planet and have chosen, for personal reasons or humanistic grounds, to integrate a fetus or an already-formed body and enter a cycle of earthly incarnations. Incorporation is usually done when the fetus is three weeks old, but sometimes before.

A physical body is not automatically associated with a *soul*; there are bodies or people who have no *soul*. But since it takes a *soul* to make a body work, they are in an iddle state, and live their life without ever questioning the system they live in or without spiritual research and are guided thanks to advanced technologies such as artificial intelligence.

• 56.1 — Stellar Emissaries (StarSeeds)
The Terrestrial Natives (EarthSeeds)

Stellars (extraterrestrials) that reincarnate on Earth are essentially divided into 2 main groups:

1/ Stellar Emissaries (StarSeeds) are: people from another planet. They could be compared to Emissaries who came from a foreign planet, came down to Earth to do work or perform a temporary or recurrent mission, for a given number of years. They choose to be stashed in medical pods operating under a computer immersion program with state-of-the-art artificial technologies. They haven't been on Earth recently, or only been for one or two, maybe three reincarnations.

Upon their death on Earth, the *soul* returns directly to the body stashed in the medical pod, regardless of the ship or planet where it is stored. For example, if the body in stasis is stored in a Pleiadian ship, the *soul* returns systematically and directly to the Pleiadian ship. If the body in stasis is among the Arcturians, the *soul* returns to the Arcturians.

2/ The Terrestrial Natives (EarthSeeds) are people who are born directly from the Source and evolve naturally from one species to another without the help of advanced technology. At the time of death on Earth, the soul that has no other body to go to may choose to be born again on Earth, or on another planet and reincarnate in the Andromedan or in the Arcturian worlds.

The two categories are scattered everywhere in the universe; it is not a phenomenon specific to planet Earth, because wanting to live in multiple places to experience it, is part of the normal evolution of a *soul*. Some people prefer one planet over others and they choose to stay several lives in this place that they particularly like. After evolving, the Emissaries and Natives will move to other places, but all people living on Earth and having *souls,* have already lived everywhere in the universe within multiple races and interstellar groups.

Many Earthlings are pure native Earthlings who have matured spiritually to the point of awakening to their true identity, which often gives them the feeling of being strangers on Earth, which they find in general very surprising. Both categories may or may not have the memory of being born in another place or on another planet, which increases their sense of alienation tenfold.

Emissaries and Natives are unique and present in all physical forms, sizes, nationalities or skin colors, but they share a common sense of isolation, as they are constantly confronted with the inner need, strongly prevalent for them, to be at the service of others and to be forced to live surrounded by egotistical people for whom this is not the priority. Both categories share this dilemma because their inner universe has changed, and the real world has evolved and has already gone from binary and 3D dual

Earth to the aesthetic and ethical intimacy of the non-dual 5D world.

• 56.2 — Birth on Earth
Stellar Emissaries, do they form groups of *souls* on Earth?
Can any stellar (extraterrestrial) come to Earth and is there a selection of *souls* intentionally prepared for the execution of missions?
Are some *souls* part of the cycles of reincarnation until they become aware of what they are?

Any stellar (alien) can be born on Earth and they tend to incarnate in groups. But many may choose single, even self-imposed or self-programmed missions. Nevertheless, depending on the person's original frequency, they may need the help of a specific technology that may be an implant or a medical pod.

In general, the majority of Earthlings are *souls* who have already lived many incarnations on Earth or elsewhere and may need to live many more, before they can awaken to their stellar (extraterrestrial) status. and their mission, may need the use cutting-edge technologies, or natives, who pass from one species to another, and through natural biological evolution. Stellar (extraterrestrial) Emissaries may need many incarnations and cycles of evolution before they finally realize who and what they really are.

• 56.3 — Synchronization of the Mother's Frequencies

At the moment of birth on Earth: the mother must raise her natural frequency by meditating, or be prepared to artificially increase it in order to accommodate the fetus. This is done technologically according to species by inserting a small device such as an implant that serves many purposes, such as assessing the physiological state of the future parturient, and to increase or change the mother's frequency to accommodate the baby's frequency. If this is not done, neurological problems can occur, endangering the life of the mother and the baby. This upgrade is usually performed by *Small Greys* under the orders of various extraterrestrial races.

• 56.4 — The different types of nursing beds or medical pods and immersion programs

How is the process of reincarnation in a medical pod using an immersion program? (Medical bed, medical pod). Where are the bodies stored until they wake up?

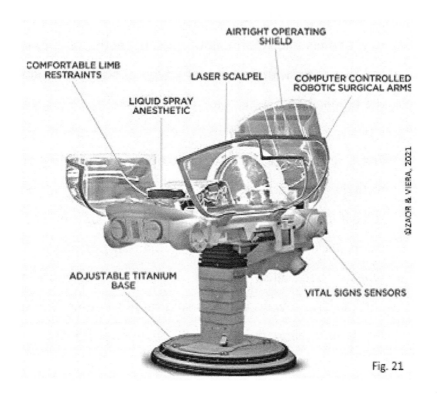

AIRTIGHT OPERATING
SHIELD

COMFORTABLE LIMB
RESTRAINTS

LASER SCALPEL

COMPUTER CONTROLLED
ROBOTIC SURGICAL ARMS

LIQUID SPRAY
ANESTHETIC

©ZAOR & VIERA, 2021

ADJUSTABLE TITANIUM
BASE

VITAL SIGNS SENSORS

Fig. 21

The medpods, the medical bed or medbeds are different types of devices that implement healing, age regression or regeneration technologies to the human body using laser or stem cell technologies. There are several types:

• Regenerating Beds •

They can cure all kinds of diseases from cancer to post-traumatic symptoms, back pain and chronic pain, kidney problems, depression, anxiety. They can repair all broken or fractured bones and reform limbs, organs, teeth, parts of skeleton, brain, flesh or to erase any type of scars or injuries on the human body.

These are automated medical stations where a surgeon selects the type of procedure to be performed from the computer database, then the patient lies in the pod and the machine performs the operation or medical procedure. These types of beds allow surgeons or doctors to diagnose, treat and perform a wide range of surgical procedures with ultra-fine laser incisions guided by a 3D anatomical scan.

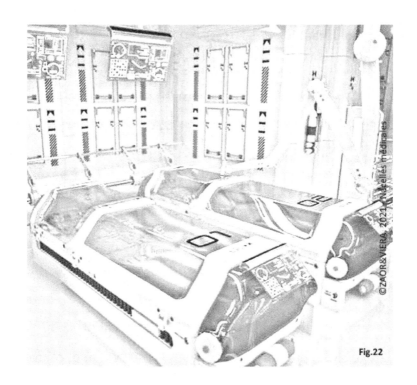

Fig.22

• The Reatomization Pods •

They regenerate the entire human body in 2-3 minutes, from head to toe, and can use age regression technologies. All body functions and metabolic rates are monitored remotely, so there are no monitors attached to the person.

What does this cutting-edge technology mean for an 80-year-old woman? She could be young again, have children and start a new family if she wanted to.

• Holographic pods •

They are used for immersion programs for the Stellar Emissaries. The person is entirely immersed in an amber liquid very rich in stem cells and oxygen and must breathe it through the nostrils. This liquid is similar in composition and texture to the amniotic liquid in which a fetus bathes before birth.

In the technologies that were presented to me, the body takes between three and six months to fully regenerate and return to the age considered fundamental of 16-17 years of age. The patient is completely renewed and rejuvenated, from head to toe, the body gains 4 inches in height, the face and body become young again, the hair and nails grow. Physical strength and speed, as well as intellectual capacities are increased tenfold. A language can be learned in a few hours instead of years; telepathy is fully recovered and the person becomes telepathic, clairvoyant, clairaudient and telekinetic.

At this point, the patient can leave the pod and go about normal businesses after a period of adaptation to the new capacities : for example learn to grab a glass without breaking it.

In the case of Stellar Emissaries, the person enters a vertical or horizontal pod that fills with the regenerating fluid and is put into stasis, that is, a controlled artificial coma, for the entire time the person is on a mission on Earth, regardless of the number of years. Coma allows all vital functions to be put to rest with the help of artificial intelligence.

A *soul* is a signal, a set of frequencies, not a *thing*. This *soul* will therefore have two points of attention: an extraterrestrial point and an earthly point that are related to each other. It is the dedicated artificial intelligence that targets a person's frequency of attention and make it correspond or synchronize with the body that will be born on Earth. The two bodies must be perfectly synchronized to match the frequency of each *stellar soul* and then they connect as a well-tuned transmitter and radio receiver, which communicate with each other.

During the synchronization, all the attention of the *soul* will then be directed towards the human body on Earth since the extraterrestrial body is in a coma and therefore inanimate.

Upon death on Earth, it will be the opposite: the terrestrial body is no longer available and the *soul*'s attention will then return to its original stellar (extraterrestrial) body in the medical pod.

These pods are stored primarily in two locations:

. in a hospital-type building on the planet of origin, or

. in a spaceship in specialized rooms about 2 miles long (some artificial biospheres are as voluminous as planets).

• 56.5 - Blood factor Rh negative (Rh-)

Are stellar emissaries that have a negative Rh factor (Rh-) of reptilian origin?
Do the different blood groups correspond to different races?

The different blood groups represent different stellar (extra-terrestrial) races and the person is a member of a specific group of *souls*. But being an Emissary or a Native, concerns more the purity of frequency than the blood type.

RH-neg blood is associated with a group that concerns certain species; some of these species may be of reptilian origin and others may not; Having Rh neg blood does not necessarily mean that the person is of reptilian lineage.

• 56.6 — Free Will

Is it possible that a Stellar Emissary even conscious of his mission, uses his free will and decides not to execute it, even if it was decided or programmed before incarnating on earth?
What will happen to individuals who disagree partially or totally and do not want to carry out their mission?

Emissaries and Natives are all from multiple planets, but there are strong affinities to one or more stellar (extraterres-trial) species in particular. To discover it is a deep intuitive knowledge that belongs to each person or *soul* who alone knows who they are. No need to look for external validation, but rather, internal. It is the responsibility and privilege of each person. Determining it is certainly not the responsibility of others, even if they are well intentioned. To need this re-cognition, or authority to tell you who you are, is a very earthly mentality that the Emissaries must get rid of to give way to their intuition and control over their lives.

<u>ART. 57 – Multibreed Stellar Emissaries</u>
Is it possible to be a multirace Emissary after multiple incarnations on different planets? Can we be guided by different stellar (extraterrestrial) races of different morphologies, such as Lyrians, humanoid morphology and Mantis, insectoid morphology?

The very nature of the cycles of rebirth or incarnation means that Emissaries and Natives have more than one recent stellar (extraterrestrial) origin and will be guided by representatives of many different stellar species.

In addition, there are interstellar inter-race agreements and alliances to carry out different types of Earth missions. Some races will prefer the spiritual aspect, others the warrior aspect, others the therapeutic or technological or educational aspect. And the groups of missions will be guided and will act towards these goals.

• 57.1 - Recognizing your tribe
How do we recognize the Emissaries and Natives of our stellar lineage?

Two methods of recognition are possible:

1 - the members of the different tribes of Stellar Emissaries and Natives identify each other by a deep, intui-

tive inner recognition in the same way that a giraffe will recognize another and not a lion, as part of the tribe. You know the adage: *Birds of a Feather Flock Together* and the Stellar Emissaries tend to congregate by lineage or race.

2 - by the law of attraction: some people on Earth may remember another person of a different species because they have lived several lives together even if it is an Earthling and the other person, another stellar species, currently also on Earth or in a 5D spacecraft.

• **57.2 - Differences between programs**
It seems that Emissaries belonging to different stellar families have different programs; some are more supportive of human interests and others focus solely on themselves. Do Stellar Emissaries also have an ego and need to be aware of it?

As long as the earthly reality is dual and the populations dissociate matter from mind or from the spiritual, or the *lower self* from a *higher self* and a *me* and a *you*, the ego will exist. Earthlings consider the ego as a set of negative traits that must be transformed while what is fundamental is the fact that it is from the moment that self-awareness is altered that the ego appears and that it is at the level of the self that the inner work must be done, not at the level of the ego. The ego wants to control the person, but in reality, it is the deep self that subtly leads the ego. As Carl Gustav Jung rightly pointed out: the ego is the result of the destruction of the self. We start with ourselves...but it is imperative not to finish there, because even if the *self* is the starting point, it is not the goal.

Stellar Emissaries or Natives may ignore the existence of the *self* and choose to indulge in it especially since they often have abilities that many other people do not have and seek to play them.

They adopt the status of Stellar Emissary (StarSeed) to mark and highlight their differences; but they often evolve as fanciful dreamers, channelers of mythical Great Masters or Higher Extraterrestrial Entities as loopholes. By proclaiming their generally telepathic links in laudatory terms with Higher Beings, they present themselves as a more or less identical copy and create a gap between what they are — Earthlings with human responsibilities — and a projection of a Higher Self. They thus create a dichotomy between what they are in the present and what they wish to be...that they will never achieve since it is a thought they project;

the more they move in this direction, the deeper the gap deepens and moving their goals further away. They enjoy it until they have the courage to ask themselves the right questions.

The only way for a society to grow in equity in all respects is to transform the existing society into a holographic society — from the ancient Greek ὅλος, hólos meaning whole (without duality) — without money, organized in Step Councils (from the individual to the collective). If this goal is not achieved, the opposing parties who have developed the present societal, economic, psychological, religious and spiritual system based on pyramidal structures with one head governance — which the vast majority of populations accept without questioning it — will automatically gain in power, influence and planetary resources, and the Emissaries or Natives will continue to have difficulty living on Earth.

All Stellar Emissaries who do not want a holographic society without money—and it is their privilege and right to make this choice—will nevertheless have to spend more time on a planet that corresponds to their frequency and evolve through them-to continue to learn and draw their own conclusions.

• 57.3 — Stellar Emissary Programs and Missions
It is said that Stellar Emissaries come to Earth to support Earth's evolution. Why do they do it and what do they gain?

The missions or reasons why Stellar Emissaries incarnate on Earth are as varied as the number of incarnated persons and there may be one or multiple reasons. When they incarnate together on a planet, they do so to carry out a collective mission or common goals.

They tend to group together, depending on their species and their interests, so some groups are more invasive than others. It's a problem in itself, because even though different species are allies and get along perfectly in 5D where their star identity is clear, on earth it's less obvious and a matter of intuition and stellar emissaries belonging to the same races, even fight each other.

Let us recall what had been reported to the ART. 25.1:

« In general, Earthlings are not considered as a species in itself, but as a combination, a biological garment, artificially standardized at low frequency, for a stellar (extraterrestrial) who would make the choice, can *put it* on or *slide* into it for one reason: to experience being a human being on Earth. »

On the other hand, from an Earthling perspective, the Stellar Emissary, which is in reality an alien *under cover*, has its own way of seeing things and considered a species in its own right, all the more unique as it is composed of *souls* of very diverse species, agglomerated into a strange chaotic, colonizing, controversial, and extremely diverse race.

The future of Stellar Emissaries during and after the transition is up to them. Each person knows exactly what to do and where to go. Most will return to their medical pods or, in the case of natives, to another planet, or where they feel most comfortable. Others will decide to continue to live on Earth.

The only thing they will really gain is personal evolution and experience, and spiritual enlightenment that can accompany life on Earth.

Some Star Emissaries aim for other, more material things, because after they return to their spaceship or planet, they may gain a new status, a rank, title, respectability, or celebrity they didn't have before in their respective societies, or perhaps a material gain like a new individual spaceship with state-of-the-art technology, a new home, or other benefits.

ART. 58 – Targeting of Stellar Emissaries

Do the controllers in place know the origins of the Star Emissaries?
Do they have technologies to determine whether they are a threat? If so, are they artificially controlled?

• Tracking •

It is no longer a secret that large databases are managed by artificial intelligence that trace and record all personal data and are updated, in continuous flow and in real time. Not all Stellar Emissaries are systematically targeted, but over the years many are spotted because of the public actions that Emissaries tend to put in place.

Genetic tests carried out during blood tests are also used. For example, when a person wants to become a soldier, the results of the mandatory blood tests will be analyzed to determine which soldier can join the super soldier programs or those in which each future soldier can possibly shine and excel.

These technologies can not only accurately detect stellar lines, but with enough data, they can recognize the star (alien) that has reincarnated on Earth; If this person poses a significant threat to the existing system, more sophisticated and specific surveillance technologies are put in place.

• Control by advanced technology •

Stellar Emissaries reincarnate on Earth in record numbers per wave, and in general, they are all closely monitored in one form or another. This is also partly the goal of programs like 5G technology and the implementation of wifi networks. The Stellar Emissaries and the Natives are thus immersed in an additional layer of low frequency control, in addition to the frequency of the lunar matrix set up for millennia and broadcast without interruption 24h/24h.

Some choose to indulge in it and they are then part of the population that emits thoughts and enclosing intentions: ego, jealousy, competitiveness, hatred, or on the contrary veneration and dependence; Unfortunately, they carry with them people in search of *Monsters* or Saving *Angels*, and keep humanity powerless in a mode of dependence.

CONCLUSION

In the Earth dual world, the dichotomy consists in dividing life into dependent and disjointed parts. At least two choices are offered to your free will... which should not even exist, since Everything is One.

Left and right, good and evil, material and spiritual.
Each side is an integral part of the same script.

The free will you think you have is only that of making a choice between two enclosing solutions. By choosing one or the other, you inevitably and continually sink into what you are trying to free yourself from.

But there is another perspective, tetravalent and still unknown, that humanity must develop: the one where we evolve, neither for, nor against, in immutable universal dynamics.

Put aside your expectations, your hopes and your fears. Do not try to convince yourself of how the first extraterrestrial contacts will unfold, where and how, or with what race as according to Article VIII of the Prime Directive, the delegations that will be designated « must have the closest physical appearance and resemblance to the race contacted. To the extent possible, the dress protocol of the contactees must be respected and used. »

The delegation will therefore be composed of interstellar races that look like Earthlings as the Ummites (Ummo), people from the Pleiades (M45), Sirians or Alfratians (Alpha Centauri).

In the meantime, prepare your written and oral presentation. Think about the most important and significant aspects of your life. Work in depth to introduce yourself in a simple, clear, honest and spiritual way.

Practice meditation, develop your intuition and your telepathy. Acquire the knowledge you lack by learning and train using this book. Nurture calm, serenity, a neutral attitude without being indifferent, a keen and curious attention to learning and discovering, uplift your thoughts towards the elevation of the human condition, so that encounters with our space neighbors may be fruitful and balanced.

We are living in the last moments of a transitioning world and we are witnessing the birth of a new era of Earth humanity. Become aware that we are at the dawn of an incredible event that will forever mark the History of our time: that of interstellarity.

Everything is here.

Now.

Accessible.

Tangible.

Malleable.

Don't make any more choices.

Be.

ABOUT the AUTHOR

Franco-American, graduated in Language and Communication Sciences and Graphic Arts, university professor, humanist and writer, the InterStellar Mediator was born 73 years ago, on July 14, 1948. Since she was very young, she has committed herself to a spiritual quest to find the answer to the question « Who Am I? »

She became a hermit and a forest monk, traveling in many countries around the world : Europe, the USA and India but also in North Africa, Central and South America, or East Asia, in a tireless search for answers to her questions, and the discovery of the secrets of the universe and enlightenment.

She was inspired and worked with famous Buddhist and Hindu philosophers and has shared the fruits of her research and insights for over 50 years.

Sri Mata/Ma Anandamayi   Sri Nisargadatta Maharaj   Pandit Ravi Shankar   S. N. Goenka   Vimala Thakar

Alexandra David-Neel   Sri Aurobindo and The Mother   Ramana Maharshi   Jiddu Krishnamurti

For five years, from March-April 2016 to April 2021, she was in open and frontal contact with a range of various interstellar species: 29 extraterrestrials, 11 men and 18 women from six different lineages:

- live audio and in direct writing:

. Andromedans, Taygetan-Pleiadians,

Ummites and Draconians

- holographic and telepathic immersion programs:

. Telosian-Agarthians, Alpha-Draconians,

Dieslientiplex-Arcturians, Urmahs

with whom she had hundreds of personal conversations from their spaceships or from Viera Andromeda, a gigantic artificial biosphere, a cosmonautic spaceport, stationed behind the Moon.

Among her contacts were:

-the Andromedan Moranae of Viera, the American Alex Collier's famous contact (1995),

-the Pleiadian-Antarian Five-Star General of the Army Rashell of Temmer, contact of the American President Dwight Eisenhower (1954),

-or the Taygetan-Pleiadian Five Star General of the Army Asket of Temmer, contact of the Swiss «Billy» Eduard Meier (1975);

she also had several conversations with a Ummite defector welcomed by an enemy spacecraft and participated, as a Mediator, in the sessions of the High Council of Andromeda within the United Federation of Planets, thanks to her mentor Zen, who was her translator and spokesperson and who presented on her behalf, the answers to questions that were asked.

On December 23rd 2017, after two years of secret and discreet personal extraterrestrial relationships, she decided to open her own contacts and put some 40 Earthlings, men and women of various nationalities, in contact with extraterrestrials of different lineages, in personal conversations or within groups she had organized.

The author's role is to facilitate a neutral and benevolent process through which the Earth and extraterrestrial parties understand each other and try to communicate. Her help varies according to the contexts of application ; it includes elements of pedagogy and relational quality and gives rise to creativity and a new sense of self, based on the principles of: -free will, -balance, -autonomy, -responsibility, -listening, -mutual respect - and -service to others.

FIRST CONTACTS is the third book in the EXOMORPHOSES series, published after *ARTIFICIAL* and 1793, Marie-Antoinette – Transmutation Cosmique.

LIST of THE 85 QUESTIONS

being answered in this book

CHAPTER 1

EXTRATERRESTRIAL CONTACT AND COMMUNICATION

Page

| 13 | ART. 1 | 1 Were the gods and mythical monsters extraterrestrials? |

| 16 | ART. 2 | 2 Are all extraterrestrials, beings of light? What about the Reptilians? |

| 20 | ART. 3 | 3 By what means do the stellar (extraterrestrial) peoples come into contact with the Earthlings? |

4 Is there a list of real stellars who communicate on social networks?

| 25 | ART. 4 | 5 What are the selection criteria for Earth contactees? |

6 Are stellar Emissaries (StarSeeds) registered at the government level?

| 28 | ART. 5 | 7 How did the extraterrestrials come into contact with you? |

| 34 | ART. 6 | 8 How did you react to your first contact? |

9 What were your feelings?

| 37 | ART. 7 | 10 How do stellars (extraterrestrials) communicate? |

11 How many are there?

12 What breeds?

| 58 | ART. 8 | 13 Do extraterrestrials affect our emotions? |

| 61 | ART. 9 | 14 Why do I have tinnitus or wheezing in my ears or in my lower skull? |

63	ART. 10	**15** Are dreams used by extraterrestrials as communication tools?
		16 Do we go into other real worlds when we dream?
69	ART. 11	**17** Is intuition directly linked to an extraterrestrial connection?
73	ART. 12	**18** Is Earth telepathy credible?
		19 What is the difference between Earth telepathy and stellar (extraterrestrial) telepathy?
76	ART. 13	**20** Do stars use the arts and artistic creation to inspire us and send messages?
		21 Does the music contain *programs* that act on our mind without our knowledge?
		22 Does classical music stimulate the brain?
78	ART. 14	**23** Is the use of natural or artificial psychotropics recommended for spiritual awakening or cosmic reality?
80	ART. 15	**24** An example of intuitive communication between an Earthling and two extraterrestrials in a military context.
86	ART. 16	**25** What technologies induce telepathy artificially?

CHAPTER 2

EXOPOLITICS and EXODIPLOMACY

Page

95	ART. 17	**26** How do stellars (extraterrestrials) perceive Earthlings?
104	ART. 18	**27** Have extraterrestrials made contact with world governments?
		28 Why is there so much secrecy about their existence?
106	ART. 19	**29** What treaties have been signed with Earth governments?
111	ART. 20	**30** Have extraterrestrials made contact with Heads of State? (Part 1)

125	ART. 21	**31** Have extraterrestrials made contact with Heads of State? (Part 2)
130	ART. 22	**32** How to address stellars (extraterrestrials)?
145	ART. 23	**33** Is there any danger in coming into contact with extraterrestrials?
147	ART. 24	**34** What would be the impacts of official contact with extraterrestrials?

CHAPTER 3

EXTRATERRESTRIAL CATEGORIZATION OF EARTHLINGS

Page

153	ART. 25	**35** How do stellars study Earthlings?
156	ART. 26	**36** What are the different types of humans on Earth?
160	ART. 27	**37** What is a crawl-in?
161	ART. 28	**38** What is a walk-in?
163	ART. 29	**39** What is a walk-down?
165	ART. 30	**40** What are hybrids?
		41 Does hybridization exist between humans and animals?
174	ART. 31	**42** Do kidnappings (abductions) have anything to do with hybridization?
		43 Does hybridization exist between two stellar (extraterrestrial) species?
181	ART. 32	**44** Are the new technologies destroying our species?
		45 How do stellars (extraterrestrials) manage biology and technology?
184	ART. 33	**46** Do human clones already exist?
		47 Do extraterrestrials have clones?
		48 Who are the clones and what are their roles?
196	ART. 34	**49** Do the Mibs really exist?
203	ART. 35	**50** Who and what are the Borgs?
205	ART. 36	**51** What are extraterrestrial variants (Timeline variants)?

CHAPTER 4

REINCARNATION FILLS UP WITH *SOULS*

Page

210	ART. 37	**52**	What is a soul ? Is a soul immortal ?
211	ART. 38	**53**	The *soul* in prehistory
213	ART. 39	**54**	*The soul* in Hinduism
215	ART. 40	**55**	*The soul* in Buddhism
216	ART. 41	**56**	The *soul* in Judaism
217	ART. 42	**57**	The *soul* in Christianity
218	ART. 43	**58**	The *soul* in Islam
219	ART. 44	**59**	The *soul* of Greek Antiquity
224	ART. 45	**60**	The *soul* of the medieval West
225	ART. 46	**61**	The *soul* in philosophy
227	ART. 47	**62**	The *Soul* in the Age of Enlightenment
244	ART. 48	**63**	The *soul* in psychology
248	ART. 49	**64**	The *soul* of atomists and physicists

CHAPTER 5

POLYPTYCH OF REINCARNATION

Page

254	ART. 50	**65**	What is reincarnation?
257	ART. 51	**66**	Does life end definitively once our physical body dies?
		67	Does human consciousness survive after death?
		68	Is death the end of everything?
		69	Where does the soul *go after death?*
271	ART. 52	**70**	The West and Reincarnation

278 | ART. 53 | **71** Academic Sciences and Reincarnation

299 | ART. 54 | **72** Women and reincarnation

310 | ART. 55 | **73** Do stellars (extraterrestrials) assess the existence of a soul?
74 Is there a tangible reality after death?
75 Do stellars (extraterrestrials) die?
76 Is death for them the same as on Earth?
77 Do they reincarnate?

318 | ART. 56 | **78** What are the differences between StarSeeds and Earth-
79 Seeds? How does the reincarnation process work in a medical pod using an immersion program?
80 Where are the bodies stored until they wake up?

331 | ART. 57 | **81** Is it possible to be a multi-race Emissary after multiple incar-
nations on different planets?

82 Can we be guided by different stellar (extraterrestrial) races
of different morphologies, such as Lyriens, humanoid morphology and Mantis, insectoid morphology?

338 | ART. 58 | **83** Do the controllers in place know the origins of the Stellar
84 Missaries? Do they have technologies to determine whether
85 they are a threat? If so, do they control them artificially?

TABLE of ILLUSTRATIONS

Fig. N°

1   Phases of sleep, 2021

2   Brain wave patterns, 2021

3   Maria Orsic (Oršić, Ortisch, Orschitsch, Marija Orsitsch), Austrian medium.

4   UAPTF screen shot. (2020).
Unidentified Aerial Phenomena Task Force. Department of Defense DOD. GIMBAL.wmv [video] - https://www.navair.navy.mil/foia/documents

5   Zebra and Leopard, 2021

6   *Humanzee*, courtesy Liza Phoenix, 2006, Wikipedia.com

7   DUMS, Mexico, 2017

8   DUMB, Underground Military Base, 2021

9   Plato, Socrates and Aristotle, 2021

10   Excerpt ÂME, Encyclopédie Diderot et d'Alembert (1751-1765). Courtesy of the Bibliothèque Nationale de France, Gallica

11   *L'Homme Machine*, La Mettrie, J. O. de. (1748). Imp. D'Elie Luzac, Fils. Courtesy of the Bibliothèque Nationale de France, Gallica

12   *Echafaud*, after an ancient engraving (15th century). Illustration taken from the Larousse Dictionary

13   Guillotine. Illustration from the Larousse Dictionary

14   Freud, Jung and Lacan. Photos extracted from the Internet or wiki-

pedia.com and edited. 2021

15   Pyramidal structure of the psyche according to Carl Gustav Jung, inspired by the thesis of E. Graciela Cimetti, Aspects psychosociaux de C.G. Jung. p. 253 - CC-BA-SA
Author: Lilyu. Courtesy of wikimedia.org. 2021

16   Portraits of P.E. Higgs and F. Englert (edited) Courtesy of nobelprize.org Photographer: A. Mahmoud

17   *21 Grammes* – Courtesy of Alejandro González Iñárritu Movie Poster. (2003). Producers This Is That Productions, Y Productions, Mediana Productions, Filmgesellschaft. AlloCiné - Https://www.allocine.fr/film/fichefilm_gen_cfilm=47795.html

18   Illustration of Incarnation in Hindu Art (published in black and white). Reincarnation AS. Cycle of reincarnated versions of the same soul. Courtesy of Wikimedia.org.
Author: Himalayan Academy Publications, Kapaa, Kauai, Hawaii

19   Plato and Pythagoras, 2021

20   The Physical and Metaphysical Worlds. Excerpt from *Metaphysicon* - Courtesy J.P. Petit and J.C. Bourret – Editions Guy Trédaniel

21   Standing medical pod, 2021

22   Horizontal Medical beds, 2021

MEDIAGRAPHY

Mediagraphy N°1

1 **Abdallah, Imam. (2010).**
La Vision Mulsulmane de l'Âme. Rédigé par Imam Abdallah et publié depuis Overblog.
[1] *Ar-Rûh*, pp. 170-171 - éd. Dâr ul-hadîth,
[2] Muslim n° 2872, Abû Dâoûd n° 4753, Ahmad n° 17803, Ibn Mâja, n°4262,
[3] Muslim n° 2872, Abû Dâoûd n° 4753, Ahmad n° 17803,
[4] Muslim n° 2872, Ahmad n° 17803.
imam-abdallah.over-blog.com/article-la-vision-musulmane-de-l-ame-60253970.html

2 **Alfassa, M., *La Mère* (2009).**
Paroles de la Mère. Vol. I. [PDF] Sri Aurobindo Ashram. Pondichéry.
[1] p. 219 [2] p.412.
http://www.aurobindo.ru/workings/ma/14/vol_14_f.pdf
https://www.auroville-france.org/

3 **Alliance Galactique & Ummo Sciences (2021).**
Communications 2021. Les Messages de Alphazéro. Réponses d'ORIAAU548. 31 janv. 2021, 19:40.
https://wolf424.wixsite.com/ummo/communications-2021
https://ummo-sciences.org/activ/index.htm

4 **Aristote (1866).**
Traité de l'Âme. Livre Second, Partie 1 (Chap. I à V). Librairie Philosophique de Ladrange.
remacle.org//bloodwolf/philosophes/Aristote/ame2.htm

5 **Aurobindo, Sri (2005)**
The Life Divine, Livre Deux, Deuxième Partie, chapitre 22 *The Problem of Life*; ([note 2] réf. *overcome*). p.853.
https://motherandsriaurobindo.in/Sri-Aurobindo/books/the-life-divine/#man-and-the-evolution

6 **Bhagavad-Gîtâ**
Transcription and translation by the Brahmananda Saraswati Foundation. § II,22 et II,27.
Sanskrit.safire.com/Sanskrit.html#Gita

7 **Baschet, J. (2000).**
Âme et corps dans l'Occident médiéval : une dualité dynamique, entre pluralité et dualisme. N° 112, octobre-décembre 2000 : Âme

et corps : conceptions de la personne. Journals.openedition.
Https://doi.org/10.4000/assr.20243

8   **Bedford, M. (1977)**
    Sperm/egg interaction : The specificity of human spermatozoa. Wiley Online Library.
    Https://onlinelibrary.wiley.com/doi/abs/10.1002/ar.1091880407

9   **Bitbol, M. (1998).**
    L'aveuglante proximité du réel. Flammarion.

10 **Bosman, A. *et al.* (2021, Aug.).**
    The International Academic & Civilian UFOlogical Community's Response to the Pentagon, US Government, & UAP Task Force (UAPTF). A Multi-Metropolitan International Press Conference. [PDF] -
    Https://exopolitics.blogs.com

11 **Bowman, C. (1998, 2001, 2021).**
    [1] *Children's Past Lives – How Past Life Memories Affect Your Child.* Bantam.
    [2] *Return from Heaven.* Harper Collins.
    https://www.carolbowman.com
    [3] Carol Bowman's Past Life Therapy *Reincarnation Forum – Jennywren – My daughter Lottie's memories* - (2010)
    reincarnationforum.com/search/55860008/?q=Jennywren&o=date

12 **Cannon, D. (1993** et **2017).**
    Between death and life. Conversations with a spirit. Ozark Mountain publishing.
    The Three Waves of Volunteers and New Earth. Les trois vagues de volontaires et la Nouvelle Terre. (Trad. De l'anglais par **Descoux. A.** Be Light Editions.

13 **Carpentier, A. (2021).**
    Le coeur Carmat implanté pour la première fois. Futura Sciences.
    Https://www.futura-sciences.com/sante/actualites/medecine-coeur-artificiel-carmat-implante-premiere-fois-51143/

14 **Charpentier, E. *et al.* (2012** et **2017)**
    [1] *A programmable dual RNA-guided DNA endonuclease in adaptive bacterial immunity.* 10.1126/science.1225829 - Https://www.ncbi.nlm.nih.gov/pmc/articles/PMC6286148/
    [2] *Emmanuelle Charpentier : an artist in gene editing.* Max-Planck Gesellschaft.
    H ttps://www.mpg.de/10729312/emmanuelle-charpentier

15 [2] *A programmable dual RNA-guided DNA endonuclease in adaptive bacterial immunity.*10.1126/science.1225829 - Https://

www.ncbi.nlm.nih.gov/pmc/articles/PMC6286148/

16   **Chatellier, D. (2020).**
20 ans après, le premier double-greffé des mains a toujours "la rage de vivre" - Sciences et Avenir.
Https://www.sciencesetavenir.fr/sante/os-et-muscles/vingt-ans-apres-le-premier-double-greffe-des-mains-a-toujours-la-rage-de-vivre_141564

17   **Clark, J. (1998).**
The Ufo Encyclopedia. The Phenomenon from the Beginning. Vol.2 L-Z - 2nd Ed. Villas-Boas CE3. Omnigraphics, Inc. pp. 974-977.

18   **CNRTL**
Centre National de Ressources Textuelles et Lexicales. (2021)
Https://www.cnrtl.fr/etymologie/

19   **Condemi, S., Mounier, A., Giunti, P., Lari, M., Caramelli, D., Longo, L. (2014).**
Possible interbreeding in Late Italian Neanderthals? New Data from the Mezzena Jaw (Monti Lessini, Verona, Italy), 9(1), Editor: David Frayer, University of Kansas – PloS ONE 8(3) and 9(1) correction: e59781. - h ttps://journals.plos.org/plosone/article?id=10.1371/journal.pone.0059781

20   **Cunningham, J. (2010)**
Rembrances of Past Lives. New-York Times. Article. http://www.nytimes.com/2010/08/29/fashion/29PastLives.html
www.janetcunningham.com

21   **d'Amiens, G. (1301-1400).**
Roman d'Escanor. Parchemin numérisé, Bibliothèque nationale de France. Département des Manuscrits. Français 24374. BNF Gallica - https://gallica.bnf.fr/ark:/12148/btv1b9063126g/f2.item

22   **d'Aubigné, T.A. (1886).**
Histoire Universelle. H. Laurens éditeur. BNF Gallica. Ark://12148/bpt6k6549027z

23   **David-Néel, A. (2000).**
Immortalité et réincarnation. Doctrines et pratiques. Chine - Tibet – Inde. Editions du Rocher. pp. 66-69.

24   **Descartes, R. (1908).**
Discours de la Méthode - Méditations Métaphysiques. E. Flammarion. BNF Gallica. pp. 22. 53. Https://gallica.bnf.fr/ark:/12148/bpt6k5477186x.texteImage

25   **Diderot, D., Alembert, D'., Le Rond J. (1751-1765).**
Encyclopédie ou Dictionnaire raisonné des sciences, des arts et des métiers. Tome premier. Supplément éditorial .--A-Azyme - Article : AME / par une société de gens de lettres ; mis en ordre et publié par M. [Denis] Diderot,... et quant à la partie mathématique, par M. [Jean Le Rond d'Alembert[. Éditeurs Briasson, David, Le Breton, S. Faulche. - BNF Gallica. pp.327-343.
Https://gallica.bnf.fr/ark:/12148/bpt6k50533b/f386.item

26   **Dinoire, I. (2016).**
Isabelle Dinoire, la première patiente greffée du visage, est décédée. Sciences et Avenir.
Https://www.sciencesetavenir.fr/sante/isabelle-dinoire-la-premiere-patiente-greffee-du-visage-est-décédee_104810

27   **Dostoïevski, F. (1866).**
Преступление и наказание (trad. du russe) **Derély, V. (1884) -** *Crime et châtiment.* Plon.

28   **Fridman, E.P., Bowden, D.M. (2009).**
The Russian Primate Reseaerch Center – A Survivor. Laboratory Primate Newsletter. Vol. 48, No. 1. Université de Rhode Island, Providence.
Https://www.brown.edu/Research/Primate/LPN48-1.html#Center

29   **Gilgul**
After Life in Judaism - Gilgul. A project of Aice. Jewish Virtual Library. Https://www.jewishvirtuallibrary.org/gilgul

30   **Gobineau, Comte de, A. (1884).**
Essai sur l'Inégalité des Races Humaines, T1, 2e éd., Librairie de Firmin-Didot et Cie.
Https://gallica.bnf.fr/ark:/12148/bpt6k650519.r=Essai+sur+l27inégalité+des+races+humaines.langFR

31   **Goode, C. (2021).**
The Sphere-Being Alliance. https://www.spherebeingalliance.com

32   **Guénon, R. (1939).**
La Métaphysique Orientale. 4ème édition. Document numérique produit par Boulagnon, D. Les classiques des sciences sociales. Cégep. [PDF]. p. 13.
classiques.uqac.ca/classiques/guenon_rene/metaphysique_orientale/metaphysique_orientale.pdf

33   **Gurney, E., Myers, W.H., Podmore, F. (1886).**
Phantasms of the living, Volume II. London : Rooms of the Society for psychical research; Trübner and co. - Https://archive.org/de-

tails/phantasmsoflivin02gurniala
(trad. de l'anglais) **Marillier, M. (1892).**
Les Hallucinations télépathiques, deuxième édition, Préface de M.
Charles Richet. Félix Alcan, Éditeur. pp. 1 Introduction, 19-20. -
Https://gallica.bnf.fr/ark:/12148/bpt6k5504396c

34   **Heisenberg, W., (1969).**
Der Teil und das Ganze : Gespräche im Umkreis der Atomphysik.
Piper Verlag GmbH
*La Partie et le Tout – Le Monde de la physique atomique (souvenirs,
1920-1965).* (trad. de l'allemand) **Kessler, P. (1990).** Flammarion.

35   **Higgs, P.E., Englert, F. (2013).**
The Nobel Prize in Physics 2013. Nobel Prize Media. NobelPrize.org.
Nobel Prize Outreach AB 2021. Wed. 11 Aug 2021.
Https://www.nobelprize.org/prizes/physics/2013/summary/

36   **Hill, B. (1995, jan. 1).**
A common sense approach to UFOs — B. Hill.

37   **Huet, G. (1994-2021).**
Dictionnaire Héritage du Sanskrit. The Sanskrit Heritage Dictionary.
Entrée आत्मन् *ātman* dictionnaire sanscrit-français numérisé, Insti-
tut National de recherche en informatique et en automatique IN-
RIA. -- Https://sanskrit.inria.fr/DICO/9.html#aatman

38   **Hooykaas, R., (1988)**
A religiäo e o desenvolvimento da ciência moderna. Brasilia : Editora
da Universidade de Brasilia. pp. 33-34.

39   **Iñárritu, A., González. (2003).**
21 grammes. Film. Producteurs This Is That Productions, Y Productions, Mediana Productions, Filmgesellschaft. AlloCiné - Https://
www.allocine.fr/film/fichefilm_gen_cfilm=47795.html

40   **Jacobs, D.M. (2008).**
The Threat: Revealing the Secret Alien Agenda. Simon & Schuster.

41   **Kant, E. (1900).**
*Critique de la Raison Pure. Chap. Dialectique Transcendantale § 1°
L'Ame est une substance.* Tome Premier (traduction par J. Barni, re-
vue et corrigée par P. Archambault). Flammarion. p.333.
Https://archive.org/details/critiquedelarais01kant/page/332/
mode/2up?q=âme

42 **Kardec, A. (1998).**
Le livre des Esprits. Contenant Les Principes de la Doctrine Spirite sur l'Immortalité de l'âme, la nature des esprits et leurs rapports avec les hommes ; les lois morales, la vie présente, la vie future et l'avenir de l'humanité. Selon l'enseignement donné par les Esprits supérieurs à l'aide de divers médiums. Recueillis et mis en ordre par Allan Kardec. Nouvelle édition [numérisée] conforme à la seconde édition originale de 1860. Union Spirite française et francophone. [PDF]. Introduction p.9.
www.spirite.fr/telechargement/le-livre-des-esprits.pdf

43 **Klarer, E. (2009).**
Beyond the Light Barrier: The Autobiography of Elizabeth Klarer. Light Technology Publications.

44 **Kong, J., Jiménez-Martínez, R., Troullinou, C., Giovanni Lucivero, V., Tóth, G., Mitchell, M.W. (2020).**
Measurement-induced, spatially-extended entanglement in a hot, strongly-interacting atomic system | Intrication spatialement étendue induite par la mesure dans un système atomique chaud à interaction forte | NATURE. *Nat Commun* 11, 2415
https://doi.org/10.1038/s41467-020-15899-1

45 **Krishnamurti, J. (1969** et **2006).**
[1] *Se libérer du connu.* Free ΣBook BUTTERFLY INTERNATIONAL LTD [PDF]. pp. 33-34., 53. jefflemat.fr/autres/90_krishnamurticonnu.pdf
[2] *Le Sens du Bonheur* « *Cette question du sens de l'éducation* »- Trad. de l'anglais par Colette Joyeux. Éd. Stock. p. 6., Chap. 2 *Le Problème de la Liberté.* §5. p.6
Https://books.google.fr/books?id=cD4EMCW9CgwC

46 **La Barre, W. (2000).**
Les plantes psychédéliques et les origines chamaniques de la religion. Édition L'esprit frappeur, p. 44.

47 **Laforêt, N. (1867).**
Histoire de la philosophie: Philosophie ancienne, Vol. 2, Philosophie de Marc Aurèle. Comptoir universel d'imprimerie et de librairie, pp. 344, 355, 362, 549.

48 **Laird, T. (2007).**
The Story of Tibet: Conversations with the Dalai Lama, Grove Press. p. 266. « *When the search party reached us, the Dalai Lama said, "they said I spoke Lhasa dialect. I don't remember, but my mother told me that I spoke with the search party members in a language she didn't understand. So that means I used the language of my previous life."* »

49 **La Mettrie, J. O. de. (1748).**
L'Homme Machine. Imp. D'Elie Luzac, Fils. BNF Gallica. pp. 48-49.,
59-60. Ark:/12148/bpt6k10558389

50 **Lönnerstrand, S. (1999).**
*Shanti Devi, l'enfant réincarnée. En Inde, au XXe s., un cas de réin-
carnation authentifié par un comité d'enquête.* Robert Laffont.

51 **MacDougall, D. (1907).**
*Hypothesis Concerning Soul Substance Together with Experimental
Evidence of The Existence of Such Substance.* Journal of the
American Society for Psychical Research, Vol. I. No5. pp. 237-244.
Https://archive.org/details/journalamerican01resegoog/page/n261
/mode/2up

52 **Mack, J.E. (1995 et 1996).**
[1] *Dossier Extraterrestres – L'affaire des enlèvements.* Traduc. Char-
let, S. - Ed. Presses de la Cité.
Https://eveilhomme.com/2019/08/09/le-psychiatre-john-e-mack-
dossier-extraterrestres-laffaire-des-enlevements/
[2] *Biography of John E. Mack.* John E. Mack Institute.
johnemackinstitute.org/biography-of-john-e-mack/

53 **Mata Amritanandamayi Math *alias* Amma**
Https://www.etw-france.org/amma-la-fondatrice/

54 **Meier, E. B. (1953).**
*BEAM. « Billy » Eduard Albert Meier. La doctrine de la vraie Huma-
nité : « Enseignement de la Vérité, doctrine de l'esprit, enseignement de la vie ».* Https://beam.figu.org

55 **MIBs (Men in Black / HENs Hommes en Noir). (2021).**
*MIB'S or the Men In Black…*UFO Casebook.
www.ufocasebook.com/2021/government-ufo-coverup-and-mibs-
with-photographs.html

56 **Michel, A. (1966).**
*Le problème de la réincarnation. § Et si la mort qui nous effraye
était un problème bête !* Planète N°30 – sept-oct 1966. www.aime-
michel.fr/le-probleme-de-la-reincarnation/

57 **Moreira, Albandes, L.A. (n.d.).**
Le discours systémique comme Métaparadigme.
Https://static.convergencerh.com/medias/5/LE_DISCOURS_SYSTE-
MIQUE_COMME_METAPARADIGME.pdf

58 **Newald, A. (2011).**
Co-Evolution. https://coev.webs.com/apps/blog/

59 **Nietzsche, F. (1878** et **1883).**
[1] *Menschliches, Allzumenschliches. Ein Buch für freie Geiste (Humain, trop Humain. Un livre pour esprits libres)*
[2] *Also sprach Zarathustra. Ein Buch für Alle und Keinen (Ainsi parla(it) Zarathoustra. Un livre pour tous et pour personne).*

60 **Ortolang – CNRTL (2021).**
Définitions lexicographiques et étymologiques de « Intuition » du *Trésor de la langue française informatisé*, sur le site du Centre national de ressources textuelles et lexicales.
Https://www.cnrtl.fr/definition/intuition

61 **Paperclip (1945).**
Opération Overcast. Exfiltration de 1500 scientifiques allemands.
Wikipedia.org
Https://fr.wikipedia.org/wiki/Opération_Paperclip#cite_note-2

62 **Parkes, S. (2021).**
About. Https://simonparkes.org

63 **Parnov, E. (1998).**
Women for monkeys, Medical Mysteries, No. 5 (en Russe).

64 **Petit, J.P.** et **Bourret, J.C. (2018** et **2020).**
[1] *Contacts cosmiques. Les extraterrestres sont parmi nous ! Jusqu'où peut-on penser trop loin ?* [2] *Metaphysicon. Nous avons une âme qui survit après notre mort. Cela se démontre scientifiquement.* Guy Trédaniel.

65 **Platon (2013).**
Phédon, ou sur l'immortalité de l'âme. Traduction et notes par V. Cousin. Les Editions de Londres. pp. 2-4.
Https://books.google.fr/books?id=AJ8ICwAAQBAJ&printsec=frontcover&hl=fr

66 **Pollion, J. (2002).**
UMMO, De vrais extraterrestres ! Panorama complété par le Précis du système idéophénémique. Préface de Jean-Pierre Petit. Aldane. pp. 314-316.

67 **Préséance. (Juil. 2021)**
Décret n°89-665 du 13 septembre 1989 relatif aux cérémonies publiqes, préséances, honneurs civils et militaires. NOR : PRMX8900039D. Legifrance.
Https://www.legifrance.gouv.fr/loda/id/JORFTEXT000000332354/

68 **Religioscope. (2003).**
France: trois sondages pour en savoir plus sur l'attitude envers les religions. RELIGIOSCOPE. https://www.religion.info/2003/05/04/france-trois-sondages-sur-attitude-envers-religions/

69 **Roddenberry, G. (1966).**
Star Trek : La Nouvelle Génération (1987-1994) - *Star Trek: Voyager* (1995-2001)- Séries Télévisées, CBS – CBSViacom.

70 **Schultes, R.E. (2000).**
Un panorama des hallucinogènes du nouveau monde. Édition L'esprit frappeur. p. 116.

71 **Shankhwar, C. (2021).**
Uttar Pradessh : Boy says he died 8 years ago, goes to old home, claims he had a rebirth. Indiatoday.in *in* journal.com - https://journal.com.ph/uttar-pradesh-boy-says-rebirth/

72 **Sherman, D. (1998).**
Above Black : Project Preserve Destiny – Insider Account of Alien Contact & Government Cover—Up. OneTeam Publishing.

73 **Stevenson, I. (1993)**
Les enfants qui se souviennent de leurs vies antérieures. [Trad. de l'anglais par **Valensi, F.**]. SAND.
https://www.amazon.fr/gp/product/2710705370

74 **Sullivan, J. (2011).**
Jessy Sullivan contrôle son bras bionique par la pensée. GOLEM13.
https://golem13.fr/jesse-sullivan-controle-son-bras-bionique-par-la-pensee/

75 **T.I.M. La Médiatrice InterStellaire (2021).**
LA LUNE – Anamorphose Artificielle. Vidéo. YouTube.com. Minute : 5:25.
Https://www.youtube.com/watch?v=UOZepLSBUYw

76 **Trebay, G. (2008).**
He's Pregnant. You're Speechless. The New York Times. Article about Thomas Beaty.
Https://www.nytimes.com/2008/06/22/fashion/22pregnant.html

77 **Tucker, J.B. (2008).**
Ian Stevenson and Cases of the Reincarnation Type. Journal of Scientific Exploration, Vol.22, No.1. [PDF] – p. 41.
Https://www.scientificexploration.org/docs/22/jse_22_1_tucker.pdf

78   **Turing, A.** *in* **Vadeker. (2021).**
      Kronik de la rubrik à brak.Imitation Game.
      http://vadeker.net/beyond/kronik_rubrik_brak/
      kronik_rubrik_a_brak.html

79   **UAPTF. (2020).**
      Unidentified Aerial Phenomena Task Force. Department of Defense
      DOD.
      GIMBAL.wmv [video] - https://www.navair.navy.mil/foia/documents

80   **Upanishad, Brhad-Aranyaka. (2008).**
      Transcription and translation by the Brahmananda Saraswati Foun-
      dation. § IV-iv-13. Https://veda-upanishad.blogspot.com/2008/11/
      brihadaranyaka-upanishad-4.html

81   **Vadeker. (2021).**
      Kronik de la rubrik à brak.Imitation Game.
      http://vadeker.net/beyond/kronik_rubrik_brak/
      kronik_rubrik_a_brak.html

82   **Vallée, J. (1975** et **1997).**
      [1] *Le Collège Invisible*, Albin Michel, Coll. Les chemins de l'Impos-
      sible.
      [2] *Science interdite. Journal 1957-1969*, O.P Editions (Observatoire
      des Parasciences), Coll. Documents. (1ère éd. Par « The Vallée Li-
      ving Trust » – 1992). p. 43.

83   **Walker, S., White Otter, Rev. (2018)**
      Inviting ET – CreateSpace Independent Publishing Platform.-Twitter
      @SandiaWisdom.
      https://www.officialfirstcontact.com/

84   **Zaor & Viera (2021).**
      [1] *ARTIFICIELLE.* Coll. Exomorphoses, Livre II. Zaor & Viera. pp. 22,
      109-110, 112, 154, 117-124.
      Https://www.amazon.fr/dp/2492922030
      [2] *1793, Marie-Antoinette – Transmutation Cosmique*, Coll. Exo-
      morphoses, Livre I. Zaor & Viera , Éd. pp. 42., 77-78., 87-95.
      https://www.amazon.fr/dp/2492922006

85   **Zevort, M. CH. (1847).**
      *Laercio Diógenes - Diogène de Laerte. Vies et Doctrines des Philo-
      sophes de l'Antiquité.* T1. Ed. Charpentier. [1] pp.153-154 et [2] p.
      465. Https://books.google.fr

86   **Zipes, J. (2002).**
      The Brothers Grimm. From Enchanted Forests to the ModernWorld.
      2nd Ed. Palgrave Macmillan

MEDIAGRAPHY N°2

1793, MARIE-ANTOINETTE – TRANSMUTATION COSMIQUE - BY ZAOR & VIERA

History, machine design, construction, 1st use, clinical and scientific trials, physiology of death by decapitation

BONOMINI, Mathieu, *La justice et la Justice dans Le Dernier Jour d'un condamné de Victor Hugo,* HAL Id: dumas-01011301, Mémoire de recherche pour le Master Lettres et arts du spectacle, spécialité Littératures ffdumas-01011301f , Université Stendhal, Grenoble 3, UFR LLASIC, 2014. p. 33.

CAPRILES, José M., Christine Moore, Juan Albarracin-Jordan et Melanie J. Miler, *Chemical evidence for the use of multiple psychotropic plants in a 1,000-year-old ritual bundle from South America, Proceedings of the National Academy of Sciences*, 2019.

CAROL, Anne, *Physiologie de la Veuve – Une histoire Médicale de la Guillotine*, Seyssel, Champ Vallon, 2012.

FLEISHMAN, Hector, LA GUILLOTINE EN *1793 - D'APRÈS DES DOCUMENTS INÉDITS des archives nationales*, Librairie des Publications Modernes, 1908 – Paris, BNF, Gallica.

FRANCE PITTORESQUE : *25 avril 1792 : première utilisation de la guillotine sur un condamné*-D'après *La guillotine et les exécuteurs des arrêts criminels pendant la Révolution,* 1893, france-pittoresque.com, 2012.

GUERIN, Edmond-Jean, *Le docteur Joseph-Ignace Guillotin*, t. XXVIII, Paris, J. Baur, coll. « Bulletin de la Société des archives historiques de la Saintonge et de l'Aunis », 1908, pp. 101-128, 224-245, 288-313.

GUILLOTINE - sites internet: boisdejustice.com. --- guillotine.cultureforum.net

L'HERITIER, Louis-François, *Mémoires de Sanson - Mémoires pour servir à l'histoire de la Révolution française, par Sanson, exécuteur des arrêts criminels,* Paris, Chez les Marchands de Nouveautés, 1831.

NICHOLS, David E., *N,N-dimethyltryptamine and the pineal gland: Separating fact from myth*, JOURNAL OF PSYCHOPHARMACOLOGY, VOL. 32, NO 1, 2018, PP. 30–36.

SANSON, Henri-Clément, *Sept générations d'exécuteurs, 1688-1847 : mémoires des Sanson*, Paris, Dupray de La Mahérie, 1862-1863, 6 tomes. – BNF, Gallica, Paris.

VAN RIJN, Clementina M. et coll, *Decapitation in Rats: Latency to Unconsciousness and the 'Wave of Death'* , PLoS One, 2011.

Made in the USA
Las Vegas, NV
03 June 2022

49720541R00213